Wilder's Work

Books

MINDS ON FIRE
What is Wrong With Our Thoughts and How to Fix it

FREEDOM
How Grace Transforms Your Life Now

Study Guides

Minds On Fire: Changing Your Mind
Study Guide and Video Series (Volume 1)

Minds On Fire: Discovering Your Worth
Study Guide and Video Series (Volume 2)

Video Seminars

"Living Loved"
Video Seminar with Wayne Jacobsen,
publisher of the NY Times Best Seller *The Shack*

"Where Grace Wins"
Video Seminar with John Lynch, author of *Bo's Cafe*

Find out more at:
LivesTransforming.com

LIVES
transforming
LivesTransforming.com

FREEDOM

by Derek Wilder

Lives Transforming, Inc.
www.livestransforming.com

FOREWORD

One does not often encounter a book that both teaches and entertains; *Freedom* does both in a manner that is subtle, concise, and clear.

Derek Wilder integrates psychology, theology, social work, and the newer field of life coaching to improve the human condition; by this I mean: *your personal* condition. Whatever emotional or spiritual challenge you face, bring it to this book. You will be amazed to find your questions being answered almost as soon as you ask them. How can this be? Derek Wilder *hears* you. The same answers that have delivered him can and will deliver you.

For those concerned that psychology cancels out God, or vice-versa, Derek seamlessly weaves psychology with divine revelation as found in the sacred scriptures. So while Derek's techniques are academically proven and practical, they are also spiritual.

God's wisdom and life wisdom—it's all here in *Freedom.*

How to Use This Book

The Introduction to *Freedom* gives you the tools you will need to unlock the treasure found the rest of the way through the book. Each chapter introduces you to several real-life examples of people, like you, who face emotional and spiritual challenges. (Derek calls these challenges "gifts.") Each scenario relates to the subject of the chapter. Each chapter tells you immediately whether or not it addresses your issue; the titles are so clearly worded that you won't have to guess. There is much comfort to be had in seeing one's challenge so clearly defined and, better yet, realizing that the answer to your problem may be a paragraph away.

Renewing the Mind

Freedom gives you proven principles that will help you untangle the wrong thinking and spiritual falsehoods that have fed your particular pain. To describe this kind of dramatic deliverance, Derek uses a prison metaphor. Like a prisoner escaping from jail, *you* can break through age-old thought patterns and breathe the sweet air of freedom.

My favorite parts of the book are Derek's dialogues. In these dialogues, Derek invites you to eavesdrop into the intimate conversations of others who have undergone similar trials. The compassion and empathy of true stories provide hope to all of us. I love the absence of what I call "psychobabble." These are real struggles of real people, set forth by the author in real words. We hear people talking, laughing, crying—and landing in a place of peace for perhaps the first time in their lives. After reading these very personal exchanges, you will be able to use them not only in your own life, but to help friends and family members who are similarly challenged.

At the end of each chapter, Derek gives you a list of resources for further investigation, worksheets, and bulleted lists of previously covered revelations. Derek employs over 150 scripture references to drive home the points of *Freedom*; he lists them in an appendix called "Freedom Verses." These verses bring peace, deliverance, and a renewed mind; they alone are a good reason to buy the book. Who knew that so many scriptures addressed *the very thing* that you struggle with? What a comfort!

Freedom is a new way of thinking. Exchanging *your* thoughts about yourself with *God's* thoughts about you is the fast lane to spiritual growth. *Freedom* is a compassionate teaching tool for those who desire freedom not only for themselves, but also for those they love.

Enjoy the ride.

Lisa D. Pay,
M.S.W., L.C.S.W.
Professor of Social Work and Sociology
Anderson University

CONTENTS

INTRODUCTION

Freedom in Christ

"It is for freedom that Christ has set us free. Stand firm, then, and do not let yourselves be burdened again by the yoke of slavery."
- Galatians 5:1, NIV

They were trapped. The sea before them, the army behind. The people, born in slavery, all too familiar with shackles and submission, waited for the inevitable. Defeat. Punishment. Enslavement. They began to believe they weren't just born *into* slavery—they were born *for* slavery. Could it be that they had been wrong? Were they not the Chosen People after all? Were they in fact the Cursed People? Could it be that the infallible God had failed them? Had he created them for captivity?

But, in faith, Moses raised his staff. God had proved himself before to Moses. Perhaps, just perhaps, He'd do it again—.

Almost instantly the people felt a change in the air. A wind from the east began to blow. Soft at first, but by degrees it grew. Soon they were staring in awe at the wind blowing across the water. Stronger and stronger, the wind pushed the water into swirling currents, until, impossibly, the water began to draw back...and then divide! Between the walls of the divided water a path formed. A muddy road to the other shore! Was this it? Was this the moment that would define their lives?

With great fear, but greater faith, the Israelites stepped down onto the muddy sea floor and crossed to freedom.

Freedom!

In his letter to the Galatians, Paul tells us clearly: "It is *for freedom* that Christ has set us free."[1] In this simple and direct statement, Paul declares an infinitely profound Truth, a Truth that God intends to define our lives.

We were made by God to be free.

God believes that freedom, our freedom, in and of itself is supremely worthy. Our freedom is *crucial* to God, *essential* to His perfect plan. He made us to be free in Christ. He built us from the beginning "for freedom." Who we are, our innermost self, is masterfully, perfectly, divinely designed to respond to and thrive in freedom. Christ came to set us free, and not for a one-time reboot or a fleeting three-day holiday. No, Christ set us free that we might remain in freedom!

Perhaps no other longing in the human soul is as powerful as the longing for freedom. Freedom from worry. Freedom from pain. Freedom from debt. From obligations. From the nine-to-five. From parking tickets. Freedom to be who we truly are.

Every period of history and every culture have demonstrated that freedom is worth struggling for, even sacrificing one's life for. From the Israelites standing at the edge of the Red Sea to the Founding Fathers staring at their yet unsigned declaration, freedom has been the driving force and foundation for the creation and re-creation of families, communities, and nations. Put the prospect of freedom before us and we'll pursue it ceaselessly. Take it away and we shrivel up and die. Freedom saturates our legends, fills the pages of our novels, and inspires our silver screen productions. I can't help but picture Mel Gibson as William Wallace proclaiming with his dying breath: "Freedom!"

You can't say it without experiencing a lift in your spirit. Try it. Say it out loud. Or if you're up for it, scream it like Mel Gibson did in *Braveheart:* "Freedom!"

Sounds good.

But the question is: Why do we so often attain freedom and then give it up?

Paul's direct and bold statement in Galatians contains a rather surprising warning: "Stand firm, then, and do not let yourselves be burdened again by the yoke of slavery."[2]

What? Why in the world would Paul waste his time saying this? How could anyone who had tasted freedom return to slavery? Surely this is just a rhetorical device. Right?

And yet we all know from history, from the Bible, from our own experience, that most people who have been "set free" do not "remain in freedom" as God intended. If we are honest, we'll admit that we're often in that number. Rather than living in freedom, we feel more like we are overburdened with obligations, guilt, worry, and all the other entanglements of life.

Rather than being a daily reality, freedom is often elevated to that elusive list of things that are "too good to be true." It's the pie in the sky, the sunken treasure, the ever-receding horizon that we don't really believe we can reach. Many of us think something like: "Freedom is what I will experience when I finally take my first steps in Heaven." For most of us, true freedom in this life remains an intangible, ever-elusive ideal.

The Prison

The eighteenth century political theorist Jean-Jacques Rousseau began his influential discussion of social contract theory with a famous observation: "Man is born free, but everywhere he is in chains."

Rousseau was talking politics, but I think he missed the more profound point. The truth is that most men and women are, in fact, in chains. However, these chains are far more insidious and subtle than any political system could devise. The true chains are not external, imposed by some outside force. Rather, they are internal, a mental and emotional self-made prison. A prison of the soul, if you will.

"Man is born free, but everywhere he is in chains."

So what constitutes this prison? What are our "yokes of slavery" made of?

To say it simply, we are in chains of lies. Lies about who we are. Lies about our performance and our role in God's Kingdom. Lies about what we want. Lies about our past and our future and lies about our circumstances. And finally, lies about what we can do to fix all of these lies in ourselves and in others. Chains indeed!

"That Moment"

At some point in our lives, most of us will experience *that moment*. It's when you watch in shock as the cell door is slammed in front of you, the hour you realize just how trapped you are. It is *that moment* when your life simply *has* to change, or else—.

Or else your wife will leave you. Or else your physical health will become unsustainable. Or else your family will fall apart. Or else you'll lose your job.

I think you probably know what I'm talking about; if you haven't experienced it yourself, you've witnessed someone else face such a moment.

I experienced *that moment* years ago. I call it my own personal beautiful train wreck, and it forced me to start asking some hard questions. Questions like: How does God work in my life? On what do I base my self-worth? Who exactly am I trying to please? How does one really allow oneself to be transformed by God?[3]

When I started asking these questions, I found that I was not alone in my self-destructive trajectory of life. Many Christians have found themselves similarly derailed, immobilized, locked up in a self-made cell.

Look around. The lives of so many Christians seem to be falling apart around us: husbands committing adultery; moms burying invisible depression with pills; wives suppressing anger until it finally explodes; men hiding resentment of controlling wives; college graduates hiding secret images; employees taking tranquilizers to handle the stress of pleasing bosses; pastors rejected and abandoned by their churches; families in financial distress.

Millions of Christian men and women go to church every Sunday, most pray daily, and many read their Bible every week. They work hard, re-commit, and then try even harder. But then they wake up not understanding why they are soaked in sweat from anxiety, or angry with their spouse, or frustrated with their children, or unhappy at work, and they're looking for relief.

But nowhere in scripture are we promised that going to church, praying, or reading the Bible transforms lives. In fact Jesus said, "If you just use my words in Bible studies and don't work them into your life, you are like a dumb carpenter who built a house but skipped the foundation. When the swollen river came crashing in, it collapsed like a house of cards. It was a total loss."[4]

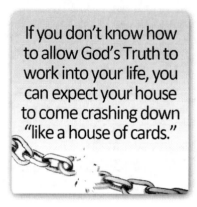

If you don't know how to allow God's Truth to work into your life, you can expect your house to come crashing down "like a house of cards."

Of course, there is nothing wrong with going to church, and there's nothing wrong with prayer or reading the Bible. These activities are critical to our lives as Christians. But if you don't know how to allow God's Truth to work into your life, you can expect your house to come crashing down "like a house of cards."

So *how* do you allow God's Truth to work into your life?

It's simple—but not easy. By changing the way you think. "Let God transform you into a new person by changing the way you think."[5]

Liberation and Transformation

Here's how it happened with me: God was transforming me with Truth that I was never taught in Sunday school class, even though it was right there between Genesis and Revelation.

Truth from scripture started to come alive. I finally heard the good news. In fact, to be more specific, *the Good News*. Through a free gift from God, Christ has come, that all who believe in Him might find true freedom. You might call it our "*re*-birthright" of freedom. A free gift of liberation! With such an inheritance, should we be like Esau and trade it for servitude? Of course not! We should fly to freedom!

What does God's freedom look like?

God's word is rife with descriptions of our inheritance of freedom, descriptions like those upon which the chapters of this book are based:

1. I have been "set free from the stifling atmosphere of pleasing others."[6]
2. "I tried keeping rules and working my head off to please God, and it didn't work."[7]
3. "I am no longer driven to impress God."[8]
4. I'm learning to think like Him and living out my days "free to pursue what God wants instead of being tyrannized by what I want."[9]
5. I "don't know the first thing about tomorrow,"[10] so I'm giving my "entire attention to what God is doing right now."[11]
6. "Consider it a gift, friends, when tests and challenges come at you from all sides."[12]
7. "If there are corrections to be made or manners to be learned, God can handle that without your help."[13]

As God's Truth is released from the Spirit of Christ in us and resonates in our minds, our lives begin to transform—and we begin to experience true freedom, here and now.

Anxiety decreases and antidepressant medication is eventually thrown out. Couples start to reconcile. Anger subsides. Divorced men and women relearn civility. Worry dissipates and frustration dissolves. We experience freedom!

Freedom through Renewal

Perhaps one of the most important questions one can ask as a Christian is: "What is God's will for my life?" We go to church a couple of times a week; we seek out spiritual mentors; we read books from Christian gurus as we look for God's direction, His guidance, His will.

In fact, a few years ago, I was thinking the same thought: What is God's will? I was given a wonderful little verse; actually it was just half a verse. It simultaneously intrigued me and set me back.

"It is God's will that you should be sanctified."[14]

17

What in the world does sanctified mean?

Sanctification is the "…process of being made holy (God's nature) resulting in a changed life-style for the believer."[15] In other words, sanctification is simply the process of ourselves (our minds and our emotions, or, simply put, our souls) being transformed to God's nature, and when this occurs, our life (our actions) changes. It is God's will that my mind (thoughts) and emotions be transformed to be like Him, and when this occurs, my actions and my lifestyle will follow suit.

So far so good. However, what does this really mean for me here and now, in concrete terms?

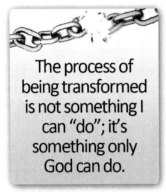

The process of being transformed is not something I can "do"; it's something only God can do.

If God's will for my life is the process of being transformed by God, what am *I* supposed to do?

Many believe the process of being made holy entails trying and be as moral as possible. Others believe being made holy can only be accomplished by God; thus, there's nothing *I* can do about it.

So which is it? What's my part? What's God's part? How do I turn onto the "freeway" of transformation?

As I continued my pursuit, I found a verse that gave me a glimpse of "my part": "Be transformed by the renewing of your mind."[16]

Now maybe I was on to something. Realizing that "be transformed" was in the passive voice rather than the active voice answered a couple questions. First, "be transformed" means the process of being transformed is not something I can "do"; it's something only God can do. This was God's part. In other words, "be transformed" could be rephrased to say, "Let God transform you."

So it's God's job to transform me through the Holy Spirit in me, but it's my job to *let* Him transform me. So how do I let Him transform me?

Well, the rest of the phrase tells us: "by the renewing of your mind." Accordingly, if I renew my mind then I will be letting God transform me, but God cannot transform me unless my mind is renewed. So then I had to figure out how to renew my mind—.

THE FOUR STEPS & "TEA"
Breaking from the Emotional Prison
Step 1: Identify the unhealthy emotion.

We are able to shed some light on how to renew our minds by looking at 2 Corinthians 10:5: "We take captive every thought to make it obedient."[17] In Eugene Peterson's biblical paraphrase *The Message,* this passage is explained as "tearing down barriers erected against the Truth of God, fitting every loose thought and emotion and impulse into the structure of life shaped by Christ."[18] In order to identify the thoughts that need to be taken captive, we have to identify which ones do not line up with God's Truth. This is rather simple. When we identify unhealthy emotions like anger, judgment, jealousy, inadequacy, and perfectionism, we can be sure there is a thought creating the "unfruitful" emotion.

Unhealthy emotions are those that are at odds with the fruit of the Spirit.

We know the fruit of the Holy Spirit, or the work which the Holy Spirit's presence within us accomplishes, is "love, joy, peace, patience, kindness, goodness (benevolence), faithfulness, gentleness, and self-control."[19] Only our thoughts can create our emotions. So if our emotions are unhealthy, we can be sure we have a thought that has not been taken captive.

This is not simply tracking down "negative" emotions; after all, emotions such as sadness may be considered by some to be negative. However, in the case of a spouse dying, sadness would not be considered negative at all; instead, it would be considered very healthy. Unhealthy emotions are those that are at odds with the fruit of the Spirit.

Exposing the Captivating Lies
Step 2: Identify the thought that is causing the unhealthy emotion.

Once the unhealthy emotion is identified, we simply need to ask ourselves what the thought was that created that emotion. Normally these thoughts shoot into our heads very quickly like lightning, or, as I describe them in *Minds on Fire*,[20] like flaming arrows. So we have to be very attentive when they occur. These thoughts do not come from deep within us; they come from outside of us.

The fact is, these "arrows" that create the unhealthy emotions *are* coming from outside of us; they are coming from the world—from Satan. Most of us recall the much-quoted verse: "The one who is in you is greater than the one who is in the world."[21] If God is in us, serving as our true center, then these thoughts that attack us from the outside are not coming from God.

I used to believe that these thoughts that were creating unhealthy emotions were simply thoughts that didn't serve me well; however, now I believe every thought that creates an unhealthy emotion is a lie—a lie originating from the "father of lies."[22] Although this is a bold statement, I think you'll soon agree.

We know how to recognize the fruit of the Spirit, or the work which the Holy Spirit's presence within us accomplishes.

If I have a thought that creates authentic joy, it's reasonable to believe that thought is coming from the Holy Spirit, which resides in me. However, if a thought creates unhealthy emotions, such as pride, envy, jealousy, anger, arrogance, malice, etc., I can be sure it is not coming from the Holy Spirit, but from the world. And since the "Holy Spirit is the Truth," we can conclude that thoughts creating unhealthy emotions are lies, because thoughts that result in emotions opposite to the fruit of the Holy Spirit cannot originate from a truthful, self-consistent God.[23]

"Flaming arrows" (lies) from the world, are being shot at us daily; we try hard to eliminate these deceptive thoughts but they just keep popping up. We have all experienced having an argument with another person, such as our spouse, and then replaying that argument in our heads over and over, thinking about what we might have said to get our point across. We want to stop thinking about the argument but just can't get it out of our mind. This is the experience of many people who allow their thoughts to create havoc in their lives. The goal is to track down these havoc-wreaking thoughts and write them down. By isolating these specific thoughts, you will start to obtain control over these lies. You will take them captive, instead of allowing them to hold you hostage.

Seeking the Truth
Step 3: Identify the Truth that will set you free.

Once we realize that all thoughts that create unhealthy emotions are lies, it is time to replace those false thoughts with Truth. Replacing fallacious thoughts with Truth is an integral part of sanctification, the process of transformation. In fact, Jesus makes this point emphatically when, in a prayer for His disciples, He asks His Father to "sanctify them by the Truth."[24] Truth sanctifies. Becoming adept at replacing lies with Truth takes patience and an openness to the Spirit (the source of all Truth).

Many times, replacing lies with Truth can be as simple as writing down the opposite thought of the one identified as a lie. However, not all thought replacements are this simple. In fact, at times it will be imperative to shift entire paradigms in order to arrive at the Truth. A shift prompted by the Spirit. The Truth comes when we open up to the Spirit and allow God to transform our thought life. And though at this point the process may seem elusive, be encouraged. The remainder of this book gives dozens of real-life stories of exactly how this process works.

The Great Escape
Step 4: Renew your mind with Truth.

It is extraordinarily important to realize that the process we have discussed so far is NOT transformation. Why? Because

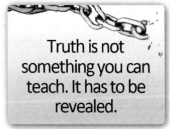

Truth is not something you can teach. It has to be revealed.

we have not yet renewed our minds. Although significant progress has been made toward the goal, it is of utmost importance that we are not deceived into believing that replacing lies with Truth is the renewal process; it is emphatically *not*! Replacing lies with Truth is *revelation,* not renewal. Revelation is "the content and process of God's making Himself known to people. All knowledge of God comes by way of revelation."[25] Replacing lies with Truth is procuring the knowledge of God (Truth) because only Truth can come from God.

At the point Truth is revealed, the opportunity for renewal commences. The Greek word for renewing is *anakainosis*. It is important to note that "ana" as a prefix means "repetition, intensity, and reversal."[26] It is the intense repetition of Truth that causes the reversal from lies to Truth to occur within us, and this process is the renewing of the mind. We must never underestimate the power and importance of intense repetition in the process of renewing our minds.

"TEA"

I use a convenient acronym to explain the way the renewal of our minds affects our emotions and actions. I call it simply "TEA." Through the discipline of the four steps discussed above, *our thoughts change (T)*. God's holistic design of human psychology does not allow our thought-life to be separate from our emotions and actions. Because of this tendency, the biblical renewal of our mind inevitably leads to *a change in our emotions (E)*. As many of our actions (especially those we come to regret!) originate in our emotions, our changed emotional state then leads to *a change in our actions (A)*. This process, TEA, lies at the heart of the discussions included in this book.

The Only One Who Can Transform Us

At this point, I believe it is imperative to reiterate exactly who is responsible for transformation occurring in a person's life. Clearly, we can take no credit for transformation; we have no ability to transform ourselves. God can transform, and since God is Truth, Truth can transform; but never let us fall into the mental trap of thinking that we have any power to transform ourselves or others. The only power we have (and even this is

God-given) is the power to choose. God's very nature has extended free will to every one of us, and accordingly, we must use this gift to choose to renew our minds. In this way, God's transformative work will begin in us.

In other words, when we choose to renew our minds, our choice "lets" God transform us. If God decided to transform us without our choosing, He, in effect, would be usurping the very thing He created—free will. And God *cannot* usurp Himself. Thus, we must do our part, using the gift of free will to accept the gift of transformation, and, in turn, we can be certain that God will do His part—transform us!

> **If God decided to transform us without our choosing, He, in effect, would be usurping the very thing he created—free will.**

Bridging the Gaps, or Why *Freedom* Exists

This book exists because of gaps: a belief gap and a faith gap.

There is a gap between most Christians' faith (believing in God's existence) and their beliefs (believing in God's Truth). We've been taught to believe in God, and yet we are bankrupt of the Truth of God, locked tight in debtor's prison. We know that the Spirit of Christ can bring freedom—that "if the Son sets you free, you [are] free indeed."[27] And yet, and yet…the chains, the burdens, the vicious mental and emotional cycles persist. But the Truth is that we *can* experience true transformation.

Most believers agree that transformation comes by way of renewing the mind. The command, "be transformed by the renewing of your mind," in Romans 12:2, is so succinct that it is very difficult for any believer to disconnect the result of transformation from the method of obtaining it. However, the method by which renewing the mind actually occurs is a very different matter. In fact, although it is apparent "what" we are to do (renew the mind) it has been very difficult for believers—myself included—to find resources specifically addressing "how" we are to renew the mind.

I wrote this book in order to bridge this gap—the gap between Christian beliefs and modern approaches to psychology. The disciplines employed in this book, disciplines that are ways of renewing the mind, have had an extraordinary impact on my life and on the lives of people within my sphere of influence.

This book will demonstrate the convergence of some of the latest cognitive theories and God's timeless, transformative Truth. The book does not propose a system or method, but instead a discipline. It is not attempting to be comprehensive in its scope, nor does it in any way suggest the four steps used here are the only or even the best methods by which one can renew the mind. This is simply the discipline through which I have witnessed real transformation in real people.

Ultimately, this book is about freedom. It is an attempt to identify the common chains and fetters that imprison so many of us, and it is an attempt to help stage prison breaks to release us from our emotional and psychological prisons. My hope is that this book will help you learn how to truly experience the freedom of Christ.

CHAPTER 1

Freedom from
Other People's Opinions

"There's trouble ahead when you live only for the approval of others, saying what flatters them, doing what indulges them. Popularity contests are not truth contests—Your task is to be true, not popular."
- Luke 6:26, The Message

THE PRISON OF OPINION

Everyone used to think Brooke was beautiful. Prom Queen Runner-up, "Most Likely to Appear on a TV Show," and sure to earn her way one of these days into a news anchor position. But a few months into her freshman year of college, things began to change. At Christmas break her parents noticed her cheekbones protruding more prominently, her jeans hanging from her hips, her wrists looking fragile. And she avoided mom's famous cooking—even the meatloaf she used to love. By spring finals, beautiful Brooke was no longer beautiful. Brooke's best friend, Anne, called Brooke's parents in tears: "I think Brooke needs professional help!"

Shelly loves her daughter Christy. She just doesn't like her. Christy is, quite simply, "a witch." She rants and raves until she gets her way, bullying both her brother and mother. Shelly wishes her daughter would act more civilly, but somehow she always seems to give in to Christy.

Kelly and Mike's marriage is falling apart. The tight-knit connection they'd always shared is unraveling at the seams. Their date nights are finding creative ways of getting canceled and their once frequent "deep talks" have turned into "shallow chats." What is wrong? Kelly thinks she knows. A few years ago she discovered her husband's secret pornography stash. She cannot seem to recover from the personal blow of his sexual attraction to other women, and meanwhile he keeps withdrawing.

Roger's ministry has come to a screeching halt. He believes it's his own fault, and from one perspective he's right. Like so many pastors, Roger had an affair. Though he's done everything in his power to right the sinking ship of his marriage, he can't find it in himself to return to the ministry. How could anyone accept him as a spiritual leader after what he's done?

Oppressive Opinions

While it might not be obvious at first glance, all of the tragic heroes of these real-life stories have something in common. They don't share the same age or sex or race or station in life. What they share is not so easily perceivable. But if you look closely, you can begin to see the dim outlines of something closing in around them. They all have found themselves in the same type of prison.

Prisons come in all shapes and sizes. We usually think of bars and cinderblock walls and Spartan quarters. And most of us would do everything in our power to stay out of these places. Cramped, austere, unforgiving prisons are designed to be deterrents, the last place we would want to be in and the first place we want to get out of. These are prisons of the body, and they are unwelcoming residences indeed.

But there are even worse prisons than the prisons of the body. There are prisons that can do even more harm and prove even more complicated to escape from. Rather than confining our bodies, these prisons incarcerate our thoughts

> Rather than confining our bodies, these prisons incarcerate our thoughts and emotions—and our souls.

and emotions—and our souls. One of the most insidious of these soul-cramping prisons is the one that all of the reluctant protagonists in the above stories share. It is the prison of other people's opinions.

If we are honest with ourselves, most of us would admit that other people's opinions powerfully influence our daily decisions. Sure, we all know that we are not supposed to be swayed by others' opinions, that we ultimately can't control what others might think. From a young age, we have heard variations of the truism: "You can't spend your life worrying about what other people think about you." Or "You can't please all of the people all of the time."

True. In fact, profoundly true. And yet... as much as friends and family repeat phrases like this, and as much as we might chant it to the mirror, we still find ourselves being walled up in external judgments about who we are and what we're worth.

Take for example Brooke. Surely Brooke knew that external affirmation was not a solid foundation for her self-esteem. The world—her teachers, friends, family, and counselor—had provided her in diverse ways with their own version of therapy. She was told that she should value herself not because of the approval of others, but because of her own innate worth. Brooke knew she should be able to block out the sense of competition and the unfair measures of beauty in her new collegiate environment.

And yet, all of the advice and therapy proved insufficient to stave off her descent into the living tomb of anorexia.

But Brooke was a Christian, and therefore she had resources available to her that a non-believer does not. She knew scripture that assured her that God loved her and that she need only look to Him. Again, she knew it, and yet she didn't really *know* it. She didn't believe it. She was like the father of the possessed boy who said to Jesus, "I believe, yet help me in my unbelief!"[28] There were many things Brooke "believed," yet in the end—like many of us—she did not really *believe*.

Neither Brooke's secular knowledge nor her spiritual knowledge was enough to keep her out of the oppressive prison of the opinion of others. Why?

The Approval Lie

In my book *Minds on Fire*, I spent some time discussing what I call the convergence model, which integrates cognitive therapy with Christian theology. Many cognitive theorists have a lot of things right in their practice. Many psychologists state that our perspective of ourselves makes a big difference to our emotional health. On a profound level, they are right.

These theorists go on to conclude that a negative view of ourselves is a certain sign there is something false, a distortion, at the heart of our self-evaluation. And accordingly, we must learn to accept ourselves, love ourselves, and develop our sense of self-esteem. This is the way out. However, it is here that we are so often faced with a real dilemma because it's nearly impossible for us to think and feel good about ourselves when we think, feel, and act so bad—repeatedly. Convincing ourselves we are good enough becomes a futile pursuit. So we naturally turn to other people's opinions as a gauge for whether we are being "good enough."

But then we find ourselves feeling the tightening of the "opinion prison," and we revert to the unhealthy emotions of anxiety and depression and anger. And again we realize that other people's "opinions" are not the answer. So often they are lies, for one reason or another. I imagine these lies as flaming arrows, an image from Paul's letter to the Ephesians: "Take up the shield of faith with which you can distinguish all the flaming arrows of the evil one."[29]

"Flaming arrows" are falsehoods aimed right at our thoughts and emotions. Brooke and Kelly and Mike and Roger have all been ambushed by the enemy, and their minds (or souls) have been lit on fire by the same brand of flaming arrow.

The lie can be understood in a simple equation:

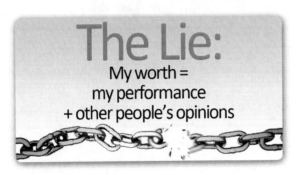

The Lie:
My worth =
my performance
+ other people's opinions

The "performance" aspect of this equation will be addressed in the following chapter. What I am concerned with here is the final factor, this problem of "opinions."

So what's the way out? How can we find release from this seemingly ever-present prison?

PRISON BREAK!

No Condemnation

In probably the most preached chapter in Romans, Paul declares unequivocally: "Therefore there is now no condemnation for all who are in Christ Jesus."[30]

Condemnation. Perhaps no other word is more antithetical to freedom. The word conveys the sense not simply of "judgment" and "disapproval," but "*harsh* judgment" and "*strong* disapproval." The Latin root means to "harm" or "damage" or "penalize."

Paul does not use the word "condemnation" lightly. As an increasingly prominent evangelizer of the message of Christ, Paul experienced increasingly virulent condemnation himself.

One particularly brutal instance of condemnation occurs while he is in Philippi. Paul and Silas are doing their usual daily rounds: boldly preaching the Word and courageously performing miracles. When Paul commands an evil spirit to exit a fortune teller, her indignant owners, who have been profiting greatly from her dark gifts, drag Paul and Silas in front of the local religious authorities.

What transpires is a striking example of public blame. Not only do the authorities disapprove of the missionaries, but the crowd, in their rage, joins in the attack. The result is Paul and Silas are "stripped and beaten" with rods.[31] In case the malicious flogging isn't enough, the two are thrown into prison.

So here we have it. Two of God's faithful servants, after great ridicule from an angry mob of "others," find themselves in prison and, consequently, face to face with the same pressing question we are asking: What's the way out?

What's the way out for Brooke?

What's the way out for Kelly and Mike and Shelly and Christy?

The answer is the same one that Paul and Silas discover.

In the middle of the night, while Paul and Silas are praying and singing hymns to God, a tremendous earthquake shakes the city. The gates of the prison miraculously spring open! Beyond anything that Paul and Silas could possibly devise, God provides the means of their release from condemnation. Though the two missionaries choose not to walk out—as Peter had a few years earlier[32]—the inexplicable events and the two evangelists' concern for the prison guard result in not only their release, but also the salvation of the guard and his family.

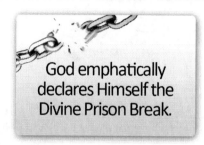

God emphatically declares Himself the Divine Prison Break.

In the convergence of historical fact and spiritual metaphor, God emphatically declares Himself the Divine Prison Break.

The Liberating Truth

So is the answer to our question indeed the Sunday school answer? Is the way out simply Jesus?

In short, yes. However, most of us are Brookes and Kellys and Rogers. We know, but we don't truly *know*.

We know that our self-worth must align with God's appraisal of us, not the assessment of our friends or family or spouse. But again and again, we buy into the lie and miss the profundity of God's earth-shaking Truth.

We know, as Paul and Silas demonstrated, that our response to the negative or condemning opinion of others should be an increased trust in God's Truth and God's reality. It's the answer we "know" but that escapes us in the cell.

"God's Spirit touches our spirit and confirms who we really are. We know who he is, and we know who we are: Father and children."[33]

Notice Paul's language: God's *Spirit* touches our *spirit* and confirms *who* we really are. Our spirit must learn from God's *Spirit* who we really are. Not what the world says we are. Not what our actions indicate. We must learn who we really are, at our core, our essence, our *spirit*.

God's Spirit touches our spirit and confirms who we are.

The salvation of God is a radical remaking of a person's identity.

Salvation Statement

- I <u>am</u> a new creation of infinite worth.
- I <u>am</u> completely forgiven.
- I <u>am</u> fully pleasing to God.
- I <u>am</u> totally accepted by God.
- And I <u>am</u> absolutely complete.
- I <u>am</u> righteous.
- I <u>am</u> completely loved. There is nothing I can do or say that will make God love me more. There is nothing I can do or say to make God love me less.
- I <u>am</u> what God says I am. This is God's Truth, and God's Truth is unchanging, incorruptible, indestructible. It is the ever living Word of God.

This radical redefining of ourselves is the missing piece of the astute and well-meaning secular therapists and self-help gurus. It is this new identity through the indwelling of the Holy Spirit that gives us the logic and the strength to believe we are good enough to accept ourselves, to love ourselves, and to develop a healthy self-esteem even in the face of our unhealthy thoughts, feelings, and actions. This is what provides the transformative power to experience true freedom in Christ.

This is what breaks us free of the prison walls we build around ourselves. This is how grace transforms our lives.

The full grasp of the power of the utter and complete forgiveness and acceptance (grace) that Christ bestows upon us is the Story behind all of the stories below. It is the Answer to all of the following issues. Through the discipline of renewing our minds, we can experience true freedom from the oppression of others' opinions.

The purpose of the following stories is to provide real-life applications of grace transforming real people in real daily struggles. My hope is that through these stories of liberation, the application of biblical Truth will destroy the "approval lie" and allow those of you who are ready to enjoy the freedom that Christ offers you today.

STORIES OF LIBERATION

The Asthma Strategy

My son, Connor, and I made an agreement on Friday night that if his homework wasn't complete by Sunday afternoon, he would not be allowed to join his friends at church on Sunday night for youth group. "No problem, Dad" were his exact words.

Of course, Sunday afternoon rolls around and guess what? The homework is not done. So Kylene (Connor's sister) gets ready to take everyone to church, while I remind Connor that he broke his commitment; but the good news is that he'll have time to finish his homework while his sisters go to church.

Then it happens—a great big frown. Huge tears start to form.

But knowing Dad probably won't fall for either tactic, Connor pulls out a new approach. Tonight it's the "asthma strategy." He starts to breathe heavily, and then he starts to wheeze like a fish out of water, gasping for the last breath of air left in the house.

We've all been there. Whether it's a child or an adult, mom or dad, spouse, brother, sister, or co-worker, there's seldom a week that goes by that someone doesn't pull out the asthma strategy.

It looks different as we get older. Here are a few "asthma attacks" you might recognize:

- "We are going to miss you so much for Thanksgiving dinner…we'll probably just have to cancel it altogether." (guilt control asthma attack)

- "We really need you to help out at church…the kids' eternal lives depend on it." (shame control asthma attack)

- "Well, that's fine, but you really hurt my feelings when you didn't show up the other night to meet us. I took it personally. We are your friends." (poor me asthma attack)

- We are a team…I guess she's just not a team player. (divide and conquer asthma attack)

I could go on forever with these examples, but I'm sure you have plenty of your own.

And How Do We Respond?

Usually we feel guilty, angry, frustrated, shamed, and sometimes even used.

If only I could get these people to *stop* controlling and manipulating me, my life would be better! This thought rolls around in all of our minds…but guess what? This thought is based entirely on a *lie*!

The truth is that *nobody* has the ability or power to control or manipulate the way you think and feel—ever! Period! End of story.

Nobody has the ability to make us think thoughts that make us "feel guilty." Nobody has the ability to make us think thoughts that make us feel as though we have to "show up for Thanksgiving dinner." Nobody has the ability to make

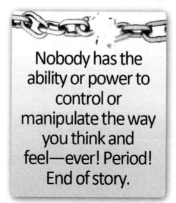

Nobody has the ability or power to control or manipulate the way you think and feel—ever! Period! End of story.

us think thoughts that make us "feel shame" for not agreeing with them, their team, or their agendas. Nope! We get to choose!

Approval Verses

Below are some key "Approval Verses." They contain the Truth; you can replace the manipulative lies of worldly affirmation with the Truth.

"Because of that Cross, I have been crucified in relation to the world, set free from the stifling atmosphere of pleasing others and fitting into the little patterns they dictate."[34]

Christ's work on the cross has "set free" his children from the "stifling atmosphere" of the world. A profound freedom is offered to us all, a freedom from the "patterns" and demands of the world.

Again from Paul—and even more specific to the manipulation problem:

"I don't tolerate people who try and run my life, ordering me to bow and scrape, insisting that I join their obsession...they're a lot of hot air, that's all they are....He is the Head and I am part of the body. I can grow up healthy in God only as He nourishes me."[35]

The center of the believer's attention is God, our true caregiver and the only worthy source of our identity.

Freedom from Control Freaks

What Truths can we glean from these verses? How might they replace the manipulating lies of others' opinions?

My value and worth as a person do not come from pleasing my family at Thanksgiving dinner. My value does not come from the opinions of my family—it comes from God.

My value and worth as a person do not come from volunteering at church more than everyone else does! My worth does not come from the opinions of church members. It comes from God.

My value and worth do not come from whether my wife likes me or not! If she wants to threaten to NOT talk to me again for a month, that's her choice! My value doesn't come from my wife's opinion. It comes from God.

My value and how I feel about myself come solely from the fact that the God of the universe is *in me*. Nobody else gets to determine that.

Wow!
What freedom! I don't have to be controlled. I don't have to be manipulated.

These Truths free me to make decisions based on God's direction and His character that is within me and you! My life choices are not based on other people's opinions or on their agendas. Wow! What freedom! I don't have to be controlled. I don't have to be manipulated. It's my choice. And I don't even have to be angry at the controllers!

Why? Because I am not allowing them to control me…they have no power, so why do I need to be angry? The power of Truth is incredible!

NEWS*flash*

> The moment my value and worth
>
> come from other people (not God), I
>
> am allowing them to manipulate me!

So does this mean I never go to Thanksgiving dinner, never help out at church, and never show up to be with friends? Of course not.

It means that I get to choose based on God's direction. It means I will *not* choose based on everyone else's directions that come from their personal desires or agendas. This frees me to follow God's promptings, God's directions, and God's initiatives. Think how many people we have allowed to influence us to take our eyes off what God is saying or doing. Think how many times we have falsely believed we have to do what *they say*, or we have to be worried about what *they think*.

Allowing the opinion of others to manipulate our actions ultimately damages their opinion of us.

The Opinion Paradox

Although the Enemy desperately wants to deceive us into believing that acquiescing to everyone else's opinions and demands will improve others' opinions of us, the opposite is true. Allowing the opinion of others to manipulate our actions ultimately damages their opinions of us because their respect for us diminishes. Paradoxically, those who embrace the Truth of God's ever-approving and loving Spirit within them will find others drawn to the freedom they have in Christ. Others will respect these individuals more, not less.

Breaking the Love Addiction
The Emotional Avalanche

Shelly's daughter, Christy, is a witch. Her words, not mine.

Case in point: One evening her daughter comes home in hysterics. She's left her iPod in the cup holder in her car and of course it got wet. Cue the emotional avalanche.

As she stomps into the house, Christy threatens to make her brother give up his iPod. She then has the audacity to demand that her mom, Shelly, buy her a new one! Shelly isn't having it and lets her daughter know.

Christy's response is typical Christy: "Mom, why did you even decide to have a child if you couldn't take care of her? Your sole purpose in living is to make MY life miserable!" With that, Christy storms off to her room, a response which is totally predictable.

But the incident isn't over. It isn't long before Shelly starts eyeing the iPod. The truth is she works in the IT (information technology) industry and is pretty good at fixing things. So after a couple hours, she settles down and does her own Google search. The instructions on how to repair the iPod are quite simple; she grabs a few tools and fixes it.

As Shelly said to me in her usual winsome way, "The remains of the avalanche were, once again, cleaned up. We all lived to see another day."

"Or another avalanche...." I thought to myself.

Train Up a Child

The conversation Shelly and I shared at this point is both typical and telling. It started with a simple question: "Shelly, why do you think your daughter treats you so badly?"

"I really have no idea. That's just the way she is! She's been like that ever since I can remember. Everyone sees it in her. I feel sorry for her boyfriend. She treats him just as bad."

The next question was less simple: "Is it possible that you've trained her to act this way?"

"Are you kidding? I *never* act like that! Are you trying to tell me it's my fault that my daughter is such a witch? That kind of question must be why people don't like *you!*"

Now we were getting somewhere. After agreeing that plenty of people don't like me, I continued. "After Christy stomped to her room, what happened to her iPod?"

"It lay on the counter for a while; then I figured out how to fix it. I certainly didn't want to buy another one; I don't have that kind of money."

"I understand. But from Christy's point of view, what did Christy's anger get her?"

"What do you mean 'get her'?"

"Okay, let's summarize. Christy walks in the door. She throws a fit, gets angry, and stomps to her room. Gets up the next morning and what does she see on the countertop? An iPod that is—?"

"Fixed."

"Exactly. So Christy has learned that if she acts like a witch, then—?"

"Then she gets what she wants." The epiphany started to sink in. "Oh my God, is it really possible that I've trained my daughter to—?"

Shelly's voice trailed off. "But I was just trying to help. I was trying to save some money. I love my daughter. I love my daughter more than anything!"

"Shelly, the question isn't whether you love your daughter. THAT is obvious. *The question is whether you love your daughter <u>more than you need her to love you?</u>"*

> The question is whether you love your daughter more than you need her to love you?

A tear rolled down Shelly's cheek. "This isn't going to be easy, is it?"

"No."

"How do I do that? How do I love her more than I need her? Where do I even start?"

Where to Start

The starting point for Shelly is the starting point for so many of us who are struggling with a similar need for someone else's love and approval. It could even be called an addiction. An addiction to love, approval, or the opinion of others. Shelly must start with a question: Why does Christy's opinion of her matter so much?

Somewhere along the line, a link has formed between Shelly's concept of herself and the approval or disapproval of her daughter. Children are very smart, and so is her daughter Christy. Her goal is to get what she wants. Christy knows that if she gets angry, her mother will feel like a "bad mom," and if her mom feels bad about herself, then Christy has a better chance of getting what she wants.

While on one level, Shelly might be annoyed with her daughter's manipulation of her, the real issue here is deeper. The real issue is with Shelly. This is the "hard" part that Shelly was beginning to recognize.

I'm reminded of when the disciples turn to Christ after a particularly enigmatic statement and say, "This is a hard teaching. Who can accept it?"[36] Many of the deeper Truths of God ask us to face hard realities.

Shelly realized that her natural motherly *need* for her daughter's love was unhealthy. That is a "hard teaching" indeed, and it's something that's difficult to wean oneself from. It's the hard part, but it's also the Truth part.

The truth is that Shelly is *allowing* her daughter's opinion to manipulate her. In turn, Shelly employs her own form of manipulation, giving in to her daughter to regain her approval. A cycle of manipulation, and all dependent upon the unhealthy lie of approval: "My worth equals the approval of others." In this case, Shelly's worth equals the opinion of her daughter Christy.

The Way to Truly Fix an iPod

How could Shelly have really "fixed" the iPod situation? First, she must learn to base her self-worth on Christ's transformative work. *She must learn to deeply love her daughter without* <u>*needing*</u> *Christy's approval.*

I know what you're thinking—that's tough to do. But with the power of God's Spirit, truly free and healthy and loving relationships are possible.

Shelly didn't think she could "Derek, I don't think I can go there. I'm *her mom*!" she told me.

"I understand. So let's try playing the 'Imagine If' game. I'd like you to imagine if it was okay Christy didn't like you. In that case, when she got angry with you, what would happen?"

"It wouldn't bother me."

"Right!"

"And if her anger doesn't bother you, do you have to get angry back?"

"No, because her anger toward me doesn't bother me anymore."

"Exactly. Hang in there, we're getting close! And if you are not angry or feeling guilty for being a bad mom, do you have to give in and reward her anger and manipulation by fixing her iPod?"

"No, I wouldn't feel the need to fix her iPod."

"Right, you won't have to reward her 'witchiness.' And if she comes out of her room the next morning and the iPod is *not* fixed, then what is Christy's next move—if she knows she can't manipulate *you*?"

"She'll have to figure out a way to fix the iPod on her own."

"Exactly! She will have to take responsibility for herself, which is an integral part of growing up, and now you are helping her grow. You are loving her! But love can occur only when you don't need her approval anymore."

◄◄ NEWS*flash* ►►

You can only truly love someone

when you no longer need their

approval.

(Or anything else for that matter.)

TEA

So what did we just witness? Let's summarize it:

First, the *thought (T)* changed. The original thought was:

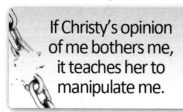

If Christy's opinion of me bothers me, it teaches her to manipulate me.

"I hate it when Christy gets angry with me. It makes me feel like a bad person."

The new thought is: "If Christy's opinion of me bothers me, it teaches her to manipulate me. The truth is that *it's okay if Christy gets angry with me. Her opinion of me doesn't make me good or bad.* The only Person I look to for my 'goodness' is God…not the opinion of my sixteen-year-old adolescent daughter! And God already has made me complete, completely loved and completely righteous. I don't need my daughter to make me any better than that! ("For in Him all the fullness of Deity dwells in bodily form, and in Him *you have been made complete.*")[37]

Then the *emotion (E)* changed. With my new thought, "It's okay if Christy gets angry with me because her opinion doesn't make me good or bad," what happens to my feeling of anger? Now I'm not compelled to retaliate in anger. Why? Because the Truth has set me free from my feeling of anger. The anger doesn't go away because of "willpower" or because of "my own efforts"! The anger goes away because of God's Truth. God does the work!

Then the *action (A)* changed. Once the thought and emotion changed, the action that followed was to leave the iPod alone. I allowed Christy to take personal responsibility for her own "stuff" so she can learn from her own mistakes and figure out how to solve her own problems. That way, I'm helping Christy grow toward healthy adulthood.

The Love Paradox

The *paradox* of God's radically transformative love for us is that it allows us to be free of our addiction of needing to be loved by others. In this freedom, we are able to be better mothers and daughters, husbands and sons. In so doing, we encourage and experience a freer and deeper love in our relationships.

My Husband's Porn Stash
The External Affirmation Cycle

Kelly and Mike have a familiar problem. They don't communicate well anymore. I wasn't surprised to hear about a communication problem in a marriage, but when Kelly started to cry, I realized there was more going on.

I didn't know her very well. And more importantly, Kelly didn't know me. It takes a lot of trust for someone to be comfortable opening up. I wondered whether she was ready.

"It sounds like there's more to the story," I said.

"Yes, there is." She reached across the table for a Kleenex. "It was a while back actually, maybe three or four years ago, when it happened. I guess I still haven't gotten over it. And then last month…but I thought it was in our past—" Her voice trailed off.

Of course, at this point I was totally lost. I had no idea what Kelly was talking about. I sat there quietly until she began again.

"Mike and I have been married for ten years, and we have two incredible sons. A few years back, I found his porn stash. I was devastated. But I thought he was over it."

"What do you mean over it?"

"After I found the porn a few years ago, he got involved with an accountability group—a men's group at church that was supposed to hold him accountable so he wouldn't look at that stuff anymore. His group was reading a book called *Every Man's Battle* or something like that."

"So are you saying it didn't work?"

"Obviously not. Last month I found more." Kelly grabbed another Kleenex.

Fallout

Kelly's account of the way she and Mike handled the situation is a common one. After her original discovery, she became upset, so he joined a "guys group," and they never talked about it again—that is, until it happened again.

The common cycle: tears, confession, silence. And the effects of this cycle are common too: Their communication suffered, and their sex life suffered.

"I thought he was cured." Tears filled Kelly's eyes, "I just don't know what to do!"

A Stupid Question

The next turn in the conversation was telling. It started with a stupid question,

> After her original discovery, she became upset, so he joined a "guys group," and they never talked about it again.

"Kelly, I'm going to ask you what will seem like a stupid question, but it's a very important one, so I'd like you to give it some thought. *Why does it bother you when Mike looks at porn?"*

"That IS a stupid question," Kelly chided.

"I agree. Most of the time, we don't ask this question because we think we already know the answer. You see, I'm not saying that it *shouldn't* bother you. But the reason that it bothers *you* may be very different from why it bothers someone else, and that's why it's so important. I do not want to *assume* that I know why it bothers you (because I've found that most of the time I'm wrong when I *assume* I know!)."

"Okay, I understand. When he looks at porn, it makes me feel like I'm not good enough! You know, I feel dirty or something."

"So you feel less good when he looks at porn?"

"Yeah, it's demeaning."

"Kelly, hold on a second. So when Mike looks at porn, you feel like you are not good."

"Yes. That's what I said! Why do you keep asking me that?"

"Because I'm confused."

"That's great," Kelly laughed sarcastically, "now we're both a mess!"

"Can you help me understand how Mike looking at porn makes you not good? How does his decision to look at porn make you a worse person?"

"Now *I'm* confused…"

Our Goodness

But Kelly was starting to get it. At the heart of her and Mike's dilemma was a crucial misconception about who she was. Now don't misunderstand me; I am not dismissing Mike's equally challenging lust issue. But the way that Kelly might help him as a loving spouse was getting tangled up in her need for approval.

As Paul tells us in Romans 3:22, 4:5, 8:1, and 8:16, *God* creates our goodness—not us, not others, not our worldly acts or our values. God imparts to us *His* goodness through *His* Spirit in us. (*See the circle diagram on page 54 for a helpful visual.*)

To illustrate the point, I asked Kelly a few more "stupid" questions.

"Well, imagine that my wife (in secret) stole money from a bank. Would that make me a husband that was not 'good enough'?"

"No, it wouldn't. Wow, I've never looked at it like that before."

"How would your life change if you didn't believe that Mike looking at a picture of a naked lady meant you were a worse person?"

"Then it wouldn't freak me out."

"In fact, your tears are gone."

"Yes, they are. But—"

"But what?"

"I am feeling better—it's kind of amazing. But are you saying that I'm supposed to just let Mike look at porn and be okay with it?"

"I'm not asking you to be okay with porn. I'm asking you to be okay with you."

"But what about Mike?"

What about Mike?

Why didn't his accountability group "fix" him?

There's another, related question that pops up from Kelly and Mike's situation: Why didn't his accountability group "fix" him? The answer is similar to the goodness question. Just as only God has the authority to provide approval or disapproval, only God has the authority to provide true accountability. Another verse from Romans comes to mind:

It's God we are answerable to—all the way from life to death and everything in between—*not each other.* That's why Jesus lived and died and then lived again: so that he could be our Master across the entire range of life and death, and free us from the petty tyrannies of each other.[38]

Mike's accountability group probably used tactics similar to those Kelly used to "encourage" Mike to curb his habits. A focus on trying to change Mike's actions through willpower; an attempt to enforce rules consisting of metaphorical blindfolds instead of focusing on his inner thoughts and his inner life. The result? The cycle continued: Guilt and shame led to withdrawal—and more communication problems!

Keeping an Open House

Kelly and Mike's situation of non-communication about an issue is common in many relationships. Kelly's reliance on

Mike's external affirmation created an unhealthy and unhelpful reaction to Mike's sinful habit. The more guilt Mike felt, the less likely he would tell Kelly the truth. The less he would tell her the truth, the less she could offer any real help to him. These two individuals clearly love each other, yet the vicious cycle encouraged by the need for external affirmation caused the relationship to spiral.

The need for external affirmation caused the relationship to spiral.

Again, the question remains. What is the way out?

Kelly must see herself as God sees her. Fully lovable, fully affirmed, fully redeemed. She does not have to feel bad about herself if Mike falters in the area of pornography again. She does not have to feel dirty. She does not have to withhold sex. And if she does not feel bad about herself, she is freed to talk with him openly.

"What if you let Mike know you'd like to know more about his porn?" I asked.

"Well…I'm not sure where you are going with this."

"Obviously, Mike knows that you don't approve of porn. Now that you know it's his issue (not your issue and no reflection on you), if you let him know that you want to know more about it, do you think he'd be more honest?"

"Probably. Wow, I never thought of it like that."

Think about how it feels when you risk keeping a secret. Once the secret is out, there is no more risk—no more excitement. It kind of loses its power.

"Yeah. Maybe Mike won't have to keep hiding."

"And if he doesn't have to hide, what happens to your communication?"

"It opens up."

"And as your communication increases, does that increase

or decrease the chance that your relationship will be enhanced?"

"It increases my chances of knowing my husband again. The real him. The good, the bad, and the ugly."

"That's true, you'll *know* him, the real him. The honest him, not the lie."

"You'll know him, the real him. The honest him, not the lie."

Finally we were able to expose the vicious cycle and address Kelly's overarching concern—communication.

Once she was freed from the need for Mike's affirmation, she then had the key to "opening up their house," an issue that is important to God.

A few verses come to mind:

- *Keep open house*; be generous with your lives. By opening up to others, you'll prompt people to open up with God, this generous Father in heaven."[39]
- *Open up your lives.* Live openly and expansively![40]

The External Affirmation Paradox

The paradox of the reliance upon external affirmation is that it inevitably results in the breakdown of that affirmation. However—praise God!—our reliance solely upon God's affirmation, through the work of His Son and the indwelling of the Holy Spirit, frees us to be open with our loved ones and to be the loving partner that is attractive, magnetic, and respected by family and friends. The vicious cycle of external affirmation can be replaced by the loving cycle of God's liberation!

Refusing to Let Others' Opinions Hinder Our Calling
A Pastor's Marital Affair

"It was just a kiss—" Roger mumbled, shaking his lowered head in a way that appeared to have become habitual.

"A kiss?" I replied.

"It wasn't a big deal, it was—" Roger stopped in mid-sentence, realizing that trying in any way to justify his affair wasn't going to help. "I don't know. My mind keeps swirling in circles."

"How about starting from the beginning?" I asked.

"In some ways it's pretty simple. I was working as a pastor at a church out west and things were going pretty well. My family enjoyed their new surroundings and we all enjoyed the church. But after a while it felt like more and more people were pulling on me. I got burned out and started feeling lousy about myself, and then it carried over to my home life. Then I became friends with one of the ladies that worked part time at the church. We were just friends. She was struggling with her marriage and I tried to lend an ear, so she started talking with me about her struggles at home. Then—"

The inevitable "then." We all know what follows the "then."

"Then everything blew up?"

"That's an understatement. Once the word got out, I was ostracized, instructed to read a letter of apology in front of the whole congregation, sent to counseling, and finally I left the church." Roger shook his head and then continued. "But that was over a year ago—you'd think I'd be able to move on with life."

"So you feel stuck?"

"Sort of. In some ways I've learned *so much*! I've realized that my worth and value as a man or husband doesn't come from the approval of another woman or even my wife. This epiphany really helped me understand how I got myself into the mess to begin with. That was a huge discovery for me. This experience was naturally very difficult on my wife but she learned a lot too and, thankfully, we're still together. But—"

Perhaps no other conjunction is more dangerous in testimony as "but."

I urged him on. "But what?"

"I really feel like God is still calling me to minister to people. Can you believe that? How can I minister to people after what I've done? I just need to move on with my life. I know I'll never get past the guilt and shame of that experience." Roger again slowly shook his head.

"Well, I guess it's a good thing *you* weren't the one that did it," I stated matter-of-factly.

"Excuse me?"

I'm Not the One Doing It!

Roger didn't realize that at the center of his crisis of self-worth was a lie. Though he'd certainly read Paul's letter to the Romans, the profound nature of Paul's insight had been lost among the external lies of the world.

> "But if I am doing the very thing I do not want, I am no longer the one doing it."

Paul says, "But if I am doing the very thing I do not want, *I am no longer the one doing it.*"[41] To help this sink in, it will be useful to look at the circle diagram on the following page.[42]

In 1 Thessalonians 5:23, we are told that we have three parts: "spirit and soul and body." The body is our earthly dwelling place or, as Peter says, a "tent."[43] Just like a tent is not made to be permanent, this "tent" is the part of us that will die.

Now think of the soul as the part of us where our thoughts and emotions live. It is this part, the soul, that is given free will, the ability to choose. This is the part that must choose to "let" God transform you.

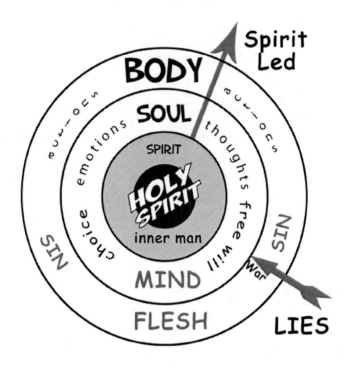

And finally, every man is born with a spirit, the "inner man." When we are saved (when we ask Jesus into our lives), this is where He comes to live. The Holy Spirit moves in, or "indwells," our inner man.

But how does this have anything to do with Roger's guilt and shame?

The question is, who is the *real* Roger? Which of the three parts is really him? Clearly not the body, for the body will "surely die." It must come down to the soul and the spirit.

Roger's response was a profound realization of transformational Truth: "The part of me that lives eternally... that's the spirit part of me! That has to be the *real* me, the spirit part of me; that's the part that lives forever!"

Let's look at Paul's verse again: "But if I am doing the very thing I do not want (like kissing a lady at church), I am no longer the one doing it, but sin which dwells in me."

The part of Roger that sinned was the flesh part of him, the sin part that is the flesh. It was not the *real* Roger. But how did that sin get there in the first place?

The answer is the same answer that all of us must face. The sin is there because he chose it. Roger chose, like we so often choose, to listen to the lie rather than the Truth.

The Enemy's lie probably sounded something like this:

"Roger, when a woman approves of you, that makes you more of a man: more important, more valuable, and ultimately happier. Don't you deserve to be happy?"

Sounds familiar, doesn't it? Like so many of the deceptions of the Enemy, the lie is a bitter pill dipped in chocolate.

> Like so many of the deceptions of the Enemy, the lie is a bitter pill dipped in chocolate.

Just a few verses down, Paul clarifies for us this common occurrence.

"For I joyfully concur with the law of God in the **inner man** (where the Holy Spirit resides), but I see a different law in the **members of my body** (the flesh), **waging war** (the Enemy shooting lies) **against** the law of **my mind** and **making me a prisoner of** the law of **sin** which is *in my members* (the body or flesh)."[44]

The Easy Part

Roger was seeing the light of freedom at the end of the tunnel, but he still had one crucial question for me: How did this all apply to his life?

That is the easy part.

If the *real* self is the part that is inhabited by the God of the universe, the part where the Holy Spirit resides and completes us, how can we be unworthy of His calling? If His Spirit has replaced our spirit then our true self is worthy. In that case, we must not be afraid to minister if God has called us to minister? Does Roger need to be ashamed to talk about God? Of course not!

Roger was floored. "I've never thought of it that way before." He put his head in his hands to hide the tears running down his cheeks. "But I was always taught that if I didn't feel bad about myself, I would just continue to sin,"

"Roger, feeling bad about yourself, and trying to make yourself feel better with a kiss, is what got you into this sin to begin with."

God's grace, his unconditional love that gives us the reason to feel good about ourselves—our real selves—leads to obedience, not sin.[45]

Our Choices vs. Our True Selves

The choices you make that cause sin do not make you who you are! God makes you who you are!

At the very core of who you are, you are filled, perfectly and completely, with the Holy Spirit. God is *in* you! There is no shame. There is no condemnation where there is God's Spirit.

The choices you make that cause sin do not make you who you are! God makes you who you are!

It is this Truth that was the missing piece in Roger's thinking. If Roger believes what Paul is saying, then the guilt and shame go away and he is free to talk about Jesus again. And if Roger truly has faith in this Truth, he will not need to look for anyone else to buttress his self-worth. He can be free of the oppressive prison of other people's opinions!

This is indeed reason to be thankful! There's a reason Paul closes his discussion in Romans by saying, "Thanks be to God through Jesus Christ our Lord."[46]

The Guilt Paradox

While Roger's story is the testimony of an individual, the paradoxical Truth of his story is universal. His guilt about his own actions, and his certainty that a community of believers would not allow him to minister in a meaningful way, actually blocked his ability to serve. The Truth of the situation, however, couldn't have been more contrary. God's forgiveness of Roger, and the separation of his actions from his true self actually free Roger to serve others guilt-free and with an even greater degree of grace and effectiveness.

> We're no longer accusing or condemning ourselves; we're bold and free before God!

The disciple John says it better than I can: *"My dear children, let's not just talk about love; let's practice real love. This is the only way we'll know we're living truly, living in God's reality. It's also the way to <u>shut down debilitating self-criticism, even when there is something to it.</u> For God is greater than our worried hearts and knows more about us than we do ourselves. And friends, once that's taken care of and we're no longer accusing or condemning ourselves, we're bold and free before God!"*[47]

THE PARADOX OF OPINION

Many of the Truths of God are paradoxes. He is three yet one. He is first and last. Christ the Son is equally man and God.

He that would be first must be last. The meek shall inherit the earth—and the list goes on.

In a similar way, the broader truths about others' opinions seem paradoxical to the world. Let's look again at a few of the "paradoxes of opinion" that we addressed in this chapter.

1. The Opinion Paradox: When my worth comes from others' opinions, I allow the opinion of others to manipulate my actions, which ultimately damages their opinions of me. When I embrace the Truth of God's ever-approving and loving Spirit within me, I find others drawn to me and the freedom I have in Christ.

2. The Love Paradox: God's radically transformative love for me allows me to be free of my addiction to love from others. In this freedom I can stop focusing on my own needs, allowing me to better love my wife or husband, my children, my mother and father. In so doing, I can encourage and experience a freer and deeper love connection in all my relationships.

3. The Paradox of External Affirmation: The reliance upon external affirmation for my self-worth inevitably results in the breakdown of the affirmation I think I need. On the other hand, my reliance solely upon God's affirmation of me, through the work of His Son and the indwelling of the Holy Spirit, frees me to open up my life to loved ones. The vicious cycle of external affirmation can be replaced by the loving cycle of God's liberation!

4. The Guilt Paradox: Guilt hinders the righteous only by moving me away from obedience. God's forgiveness of me and the separation of my actions from my true self free me to serve others guilt-free—and with an even greater degree of grace, power, and effectiveness.

Martin Luther's testimony revolves around the key paradox of God that is at the heart of all the Truths of this chapter. The simple version goes something like this: "By faith in Christ we *are* good before we *do* good."[48]

In other words, we cannot perform our way into being good. When we come to the point that we feel we are already good enough because of the saving grace of Christ in us, we are free to move away from sin, toward obedience. Grace moves us to obedience, while the law moves us toward sin.[49] Being deemed good by God allows you to truly do good. The righteousness of Christ frees us up from the prison of opinions and allows us to enjoy the freedom of God's complete and total approval of us!

THE FOUR STEPS & TEA

To sum up, the key to breaking from the emotional prison of the opinion of others is summarized in four steps:

1. *Identify the unhealthy emotion.*
2. *Identify the unhealthy thought.*
3. *Identify the Truth.*
4. *Renew your mind.*

When you renew your mind through His timeless and infallible Truth, you will experience transformation from God in both your emotions and your behavior:

T: When your thoughts change, then…

E: your emotions will change, then…

A: your actions will change.

It is for freedom that Christ set us free. God designed us for freedom. Embrace His perfect plan and experience the emotional and spiritual freedom through the renewal of your mind.

Additional Resources

Free "Four Step" worksheets are available from the downloads menu on the LivesTransforming.com website to guide you to freedom!

CHAPTER 2

Freedom from Failure

> *"For through the law I died to the law so that I might live for God. I have been crucified with Christ and I no longer live, but Christ lives in me. The life I live in the body, I live by faith in the Son of God, who loved me and gave himself for me."*
> - Galatians 2:19 - 20

THE PRISON OF PERFORMANCE

The Guilt

"Why didn't I do something earlier?" Peter was another guilt-ridden pastor. He had just received news about a couple he had married earlier that year. They were separating. He felt, no, he *knew,* that if he had only done a better job of counseling them, their marriage would probably be okay. To make matters worse, the couple had a two-month old child. Now that child might be subjected to growing up without ever seeing his mother and father really together.

Peter could feel the familiar anger building inside him. He could feel the same old weight settling heavily on his shoulders. The weight of guilt and the burden of self-blame. He had played a pivotal role in screwing up two people's lives—now three!

Then there's Sam. Sam's effort to sustain the torrid pace necessary to keep up with the growth of his company was unbearable. Sam's family life was suffering, his job was suffering, and he felt as though he were letting everyone down. But this morning had been the final straw. Sam went into the office just before daybreak and retrieved his messages. Once again there was a phone message from a concerned customer, nothing out of the ordinary. However, for Sam, something *was* different this time; it was as if the customer's voice sucked the last ounce of emotional energy out of his life.

As Sam pressed the save button on his voicemail and placed the receiver on its cradle, he felt a tear fall to his cheek. He hadn't cried in years. Not only was Sam letting his family and peers down, he was also letting himself down. Emotionally drained, Sam turned to his laptop to write his letter of resignation.

Peter and Sam's stories share a common theme: Both men are shouldering a heavy burden; both are yoked, emotionally and psychologically; both are *un*free. Their burden and their prison is all about performance.

Paul's "Perfect" Dead End

The Apostle Paul experienced the dangers of trying to be perfect. His intense studies of the Mosaic Law had made him a "Pharisee of Pharisees," *the* authority on God's Law and, consequently, any "heretical doctrine"—which is what Christianity was purported to be at that time. He had sought perfection in his profession, and indeed his peers considered him close to perfect.

But on a well-traveled road, Paul's studies in perfection came face to face with True Perfection. And everything changed. Paul found himself staring the one perfect man in the face—and it blinded him. Paul's human eyes could not handle the sight of flawlessness. For Paul, this was the dead end for any perfectionism based on his own power. Instead, this was the new "way of Life" in the grace of Christ's perfection.

Before his conversion, Paul's definition of "living perfectly" could be more precisely summarized as "perfectly following the Law of Moses." Paul had committed himself to the zealous pursuit of this form of perfectionism; but ultimately it failed. As he says himself, "I tried keeping rules and working my head off to please God, <u>and it didn't work</u>."[50]

"I tried keeping rules and working my head off to please God, and it didn't work."

Sound familiar?

Many of us have felt the same overwhelming pressure of performance. Many of us have tried this perfectionist approach to life and found that "working our heads off" is an apt description indeed. At some point, we performance addicts (I was certainly one!) feel that our minds have strayed from where they should be into places they should never go, that our brains are working in a way that is unnatural.

The truth is, basing our value and worth on performance *will* drive us out of our minds. I know, I've been there, as so many people have.

When we have extreme expectations of ourselves, what inevitably follows is an extreme sense of disappointment. We are utterly let down when those expectations are not (*because they cannot be*) met.

PRISON BREAK!
Giving Up

It would be helpful to look at Paul's full statement about his psychological wrestling match and finally his freedom from the performance trap: "So I quit being a 'law man' (trying be good enough for God) so that I could be God's man. Christ's life showed me how and enabled me to do it."

How did Paul stop being a law man? How do we get out of the performance trap? He tells us how:

"I identified myself completely with him. (And stopped identifying my value and worth with my performance.) Indeed, I have been crucified with Christ. My ego is no longer central. It is no longer important that I appear righteous before you or have your good opinion, and I am no longer driven to impress God."[51]

Like Peter and Sam in the stories above, Paul found that his impossible struggle to attain value and worth through his own good works was ultimately unsustainable. He came to recognize it as a pinnacle that was unreachable.

He had discovered the first part of the lie that might be called "the spiritual equation for the performance trap." The equation is prevalent throughout scripture.

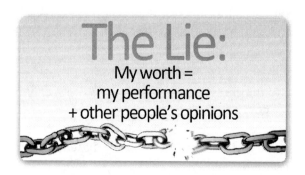

The Lie:
My worth =
my performance
+ other people's opinions

Take, for instance, this line from Hebrews:

"If perfection could have been attained through the Levitical priesthood (for on the basis of it the law was given to the people), why was there still need for another priest to come—one in the order of Melchizedek, not in the order of Aaron?"[52]

Not even the priests of God could perform well enough, much less the average Joe (or Peter or Sam). No, a "perfect" Priest was needed.

Paul says something similar about the Law of Moses in the third chapter of Galatians: "Its [the Law's] purpose was to make obvious to everyone that we are, in ourselves, out of right relationship with God, and therefore to show us the futility of devising some religious system for getting, by our own efforts, what we can only get by waiting in faith for God to complete His promise. *For if any kind of rule-keeping (performing) had power to create life in us, we would certainly have gotten it by this time.*"[53]

Did you catch that? The futility of our own efforts to fend off the eventual letdown. Like so many well-intentioned believers, Paul found himself on a roller coaster of good works and righteousness. He was driven to perform himself into being good enough to please God. But that performance didn't, and doesn't ever, work. Eventually, mercifully, Paul was forced to submit, to *give up*, and to recognize that the true source of his worth never came from his performance.

"If a living relationship with God could come by rule-keeping, then Christ died unnecessarily."

"Christ lives in me. The life you see me living is not mine, but it is lived by faith in the Son of God, who loved me and gave Himself for me. I am not going to go back on that. Is it not clear to you that to go back to that old rule-keeping, peer-pleasing religion would be an abandonment of everything personal and free in my relationship with God? I refuse to do that, to repudiate God's grace. *If a living relationship with God could come by rule-keeping, then Christ died unnecessarily.* "[54]

Paul nails the issue to the Cross. The maddeningly disappointing and ultimately futile pursuit of perfection flies in the face of Christ's perfect gift of grace.

The Purpose of the Law

The New Testament authors, like Paul and the writer of Hebrews, explain the purpose of the Law clearly. God gave us the Ten Commandments and all the other laws in order to show us the futility of our efforts to <u>perfectly</u> follow them. He proves the perfection game, in the end, is just a con-game by allowing us to "attempt" to follow the law...something that is absolutely, 100% impossible for *us* to do.

"For the creation was *subjected to* futility, not willingly, but *because of Him who subjected it*, in *hope* that the creation itself (that's us) also will be *set free from its slavery* to corruption into the *freedom* of the glory of the *children of God*."[55]

This futile attempt of living life attempting to find our value and worth from our performance will lead to letdown, exacerbation, and, hopefully, eventually, *letting go*. The profound realization awaiting us at the end of this performance roller coaster is that it is *God* who creates our value...never how well we *perform*.

In the end, the Law is based on a belief system that says if we *do good* then we will *be good* people. But as children of God we are freed from the Law and able to live under grace. This new covenant of grace transforms our very nature and replaces the "futile equation" of seeking value and worth through our own effort to "be good."

Grace is based on a belief system that says if we *are good* then out of that goodness we will *do good.*

How do we become good? By becoming God's children, through putting our faith in His Son and being indwelled by His Spirit! When God is in us, when His goodness is in us, the very core of who we are, our spirit, becomes good. He is in us and He is good, thus we are good. We are great!

Performance Lies / Performance Truths

The world floods us with lies about our performance. Perhaps no other psychological prison is so multifaceted. Here are a few lies you might recognize.

A Few Common Performance Lies:

- I cannot be useful to God unless my life is completely in control.

- People won't respect me if they know my faults.

- I must earn God's love.

- It is my Christian duty to meet the needs of others.

- I'm only as good as what I do.

- If I'm not the best, then I'm not good enough.

- If I fail at work or at home, that means I'm a failure.

- I *can* have it all.

- The more money I make, the happier I'll be.

- I have to be great in at least one thing to be worth anything.

I'm not as important as someone who performs at a higher level than me.

Lies like these hound us at every turn, and they have a loud bark! They can also be overwhelming; sometimes we feel we are spinning in circles trying to fend off the seemingly endless pack of performance lies. At these times, we must seek God's liberating Truth all the more vigilantly. Here are just a few of those Truths:

A Few Practical Performance Truths:[56]

It's good to make mistakes because then I learn. In fact, I don't "really" learn *unless* I make mistakes.

No one can avoid making mistakes (although we sometimes "literally" die trying)—and since it's going to happen in any case, I may as well accept it and learn from my mistakes.

Recognizing my mistakes (especially when gently prompted by the Spirit) helps me to adjust the rudder on my ship.

If I fear making mistakes, I become paralyzed. Since making mistakes is inevitable, I've decided to try more things and make more mistakes so I learn faster. And I might as well enjoy the learning along the way.

Most people don't get mad at us when we make mistakes (and if they do…I'm not living to please them anyway). In fact, most people feel uncomfortable around so-called "perfect" people.

At the heart of all of these Truths is a more profound Truth: God Himself is our righteousness; God Himself is our goodness. Our actions are unrequired, pressure-free responses to the gracious gift of Himself!

The paradoxical Truth is that the more we focus on our performance, the worse our performance is. The more we try to attain perfection in one area, the more we allow our lives to unravel in others. The faster we run, the more we realize that we're chasing our own tail.

> The paradoxical Truth is that the more we focus on our performance, the worse our performance is.

This is the life of the Law, in which we are perpetually striving to *do good* that we might finally *be good* in the sight of God. This futility is not God's intention for our lives.

God's intention is that we be free of the futile rat-maze of performance. His intention is that *we be free to respond to Him out of love, not out of pressure to perform.* The "futile equation" of seeking our value and worth through works is replaced by grace, which is where God *makes us good* through his Son and Spirit, and out of that goodness, His goodness, we are finally free to *do right.*

But let's not leave the Truth in theological theory. Let's see it work its real-life miracles as it liberates real people here and now!

STORIES OF LIBERATION
The Performance Roller Coaster
Rethinking Resignation

Sam's resignation letter was the exclamation point at the end of a list of what he believed were personal failures. Many of us resign (literally or figuratively) from important things in our lives. Sam, like so many of us, felt the claustrophobic confines of the performance prison.

My conversation with Sam illuminated several common lies.

"I've let everyone down, including myself," said Sam. "I'm ashamed to even go to the office anymore."

"Why do you think you've let everyone down?" I asked. "Obviously, I haven't been performing well enough. I got behind in my work and frustrated my customers; thus, I worked more hours, which, in turn, frustrated my family. It's a vicious cycle," explained Sam.

I decided to ask another one of those stupid questions: "Why does it bother you so much that you haven't performed well?"

Sam looked confused, even perturbed. "That's kind of a stupid question...of course I should be able to do my job and take care of my customers and not run my life out of control."

"Have you been able to do your job in the past?"

"Of course. In fact, I was one of the highest performers last year," replied Sam.

"Then why haven't you performed lately?"

"Volume," said Sam. "Our company has never had this much growth before."

"So, *should* you be able to do your job?"

Sam's expectations for himself were a not-so-subtle form of perfectionism. For Sam, the question was actually startling, difficult to even grasp. His reaction was evidence of how far his expectations of himself had gone, but he started to see my point.

"I don't know, maybe I *shouldn't* be able to do my job, at least not with this much volume," said Sam. He slowly began to see that maybe there were less extreme options he could consider, that maybe resignation wasn't the answer.

"I could ask for help; maybe some of my teammates aren't as busy and they could take some of my load. Also, I could train people around me, which might decrease my load. And I could ask my boss if she has any ideas on how I could work more efficiently. Who knows?—Maybe we could simply hire more people. If there's more growth, you would think there'd be enough funds for additional staff."

So it seemed that there might be a more reasonable response to Sam's performance problem. But there was a roadblock. For any of these "resignation alternatives" to work, Sam would have to do something he found distasteful: He'd have to ask for help.

"Have you ever mentioned any of these ideas to anyone in your organization?" I asked.

"No. I always felt kind of *scared*. If I asked for help it would mean that I had *failed*," said Sam.

"Why?"

"Because I thought I'd be more *valuable* to the company if I *never failed*, so I always tried to act like everything was okay, until I couldn't take it any longer," replied Sam.

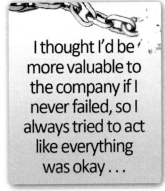

I thought I'd be more valuable to the company if I never failed, so I always tried to act like everything was okay . . .

"So you were *afraid to fail* because you equated your value to your performance?"

"Exactly, and *since I was afraid to fail, I didn't ask for help*," said Sam.

"If the company continues to grow, is it possible for you to do all the additional responsibilities?"

"No," admitted Sam.

"Thus, as long as the company is growing, it looks like you have to 'fail' at your job and ask for help."

"Yeah," said Sam.

"So, would it be okay to fail?"

"It looks like failing is crucial to growth!" said Sam.

"I agree. Now what do you think would have happened if you weren't afraid of failing?"

"I would have been able to ask for help, which would have given additional opportunities for other employees in the company, and possibly for additional staff. It also would have served our customers better. And, ultimately, I could have stayed in control of my life," replied Sam.

"And by resigning—?"

Actually, I would have been failing my company. Wow. It's amazing how deceiving the Enemy can be."

Getting Off the Performance Roller Coaster

Sam shook his head. It now seemed obvious to him that there were significant dangers to equating your value or worth with your performance.

One danger is the roller coaster ride that your emotions take. When things go well, you feel great, but when the business has challenges, you take it personally and feel terrible. Besides, when you equate your value to your performance, it's easy to neglect other important areas of your life. That is because the "high" you feel when things are going well consumes you. And the biggest danger is that we don't ask for help because we think we need to prove we aren't failures. That's when our lives can get out of control and we risk destroying our jobs, our emotions, our families.

Sam needed to replace the performance lie with the freedom of his new standing with God. Like Paul, he needed to say, "It is no longer important that I appear righteous before you or have your good opinion, and I am no longer driven to impress God."[57] Like Paul, Sam found that his impossible expectations of himself were ultimately futile. He had learned about the lie equation the hard way.

Like Paul, Sam found himself on a roller coaster of good works, trying to please everyone. But, as with Paul, the intervention of God's mercy forced Sam to *give up* and recognize the true source of his worth and potential—Christ *in him*, the life of Christ living through him by faith.[58] Sam was ready to be set free from the slavery of performance.

I'm Doing *My* Part!

Debbie's exasperation shot though my cell phone: "*Selfish*? I'm a lot of things but I'm *not* selfish! That's the whole problem! I do everything—cooking, cleaning, laundry—and that's just the beginning. I have everything ready for my husband when he gets home and what do I get in return? A grunt! It's like I don't even exist anymore!"

"So you think that—"

"And how long am I supposed to put up with this?" Debbie interrupted, "I've read all the *needs* books—*His Needs, Her Needs*, the *Five Love Languages*—lots of them, and honestly, *his* needs are getting met. Believe me, it's me that's getting left out! Selfishness is the furthest thing from my life!"

"So it's not fair?"

"Fair? It hasn't been fair for years. I am constantly looking out for him and what he wants, unconditionally loving him, and in return I get a grunt. I really don't know how much longer I can take this."

> I've read all the 'needs' books, and honestly, his needs are getting met. Believe me, it's me that's getting left out!

"Are you saying that you wouldn't mind doing all these things as long as your husband did his part?"

"Yeah, I guess, but he makes it so hard."

"So as long as he antes up a little, then you wouldn't mind doing all these things for him?"

"No, I wouldn't."

"Okay, so if you do what he wants and he does what you want, then—"

"Derek, that sounds horrible! That's not what I mean. I do love him, you know. I just want a little acknowledgment, a little encouragement. Is that too much to ask?" Debbie's voice trailed off as she realized what she was saying.

"It sounds like you've discovered why you are working so hard."

"Yeah," she said softly, "*I'm working my head off and doing everything I can to try and get him to give me something.* Encouragement. Acknowledgment. Support."

"And…"

"And that's selfish of *me*. I have *never* thought of it like that before but—"

"Actually, Debbie, it's a pretty common phenomenon.

"What do you mean?"

"It's even more common in our relationship with God."

"God?"

"Absolutely. The Enemy attempts to deceive us into thinking that *if we do enough for God, we can manipulate Him into giving us something back, or more of something we want*, something like—"

"Love." Debbie sighed.

A Chess Match with God

William was trying to hold back his tears as he sat inside my car in the parking lot near the golf course where I live. That was the nearest place we could meet when he called and let me know he needed to talk.

"I've been a pastor for twenty-three years. I've given my whole life to God and this is what I get for it!"

"Bring me up to date, William."

"It won't take long. My wife had an affair and left me. Of course, my church hates divorce so I got this letter in the mail today from the president of our denomination." William threw the letter across the front seat of my car and it landed on my lap. I didn't have to open it to predict the words that would be couched in extreme "kindness," communicating the termination of his employment because it "would be best for everyone involved."

"I've done everything I could possibly do for God and this is the thanks I get!"

"William, maybe it's time to stop doing things for God."

"What? What are you talking about?"

"It sounds like you've been doing things for God your whole life—why is that?"

"It's what I'm supposed to do. God's promises are true. I want to live in His blessings."

"Are you saying you are doing stuff for God to try and get Him to bless you?"

"NO! Well, I don't know—maybe. What the heck—I have no idea what to think!"

A New Kind of Love

"What if you didn't have to do something for God to get him to like you more? What if He already loved you the way you are right now?" I asked.

"How can He? I'm a mess. Sin has totally messed up my life."

"Sin is like a disease that we are born with. In other words, imagine that you just found out your six-year-old daughter was diagnosed with an incurable

> What if you didn't have to do something for God to get him to like you more?

75

cancer that she was born with. Would you love her less?"

"Are you crazy? I wouldn't love her less; it would endear me to her more!"

"Imagine if you had a Father like that."

"I do, don't I?"

"Yes."

"So tell me, *what* would your six-year-old daughter with cancer have to *do* to make you love her more?"

"Nothing."

"Exactly!"

"So you are saying I can do whatever I want?"

"Yes."

"That can't be right."

"Why not?"

"Because that would be a license to sin?"

"So you think if God loves you less, you will sin less?"

"I don't know. I've never thought of that before."

"William, the Enemy's goal is to attempt to deceive us into believing the *lie* that "if God loves you less, you will sin less," but the opposite is actually true.

NEWS*flash*

We sin because we don't understand

how much we are loved

by our Father.

The Alternate Reality: Freedom from Performance

Imagine if I, personally, had truly understood years ago how deeply God loved me, if I had understood that I didn't have to try and *do* better to be loved more, if I already had all the Love of the universe in me. Would I have ignored my wife and kids and health? Would I have felt compelled to *do* more and work harder in order to feel more accepted and more loved?

No. My sin of *workaholism* would have subsided…I would have sinned less! When the workaholism is lessened, we can love our family more.

Imagine if a spouse truly understood how deeply she was loved by her Father—completely loved with all the Love of God in her and nothing she did would make her feel more love. Would she selfishly have to manipulate her husband to love her more, *fearing* that she wasn't being loved enough? Her sin of *selfishness* would subside; she would sin less! And with less selfishness there would be more love for her husband.

Imagine if your child understood how deeply he was loved by his Father and nothing that he did could cause that love to be less. Would he have to lie to cover a mistake that might make him be less loved? No. Because the love doesn't disappear if he lies. He's free to tell the truth because he's no longer *afraid* of losing love. His sin of *lying* would subside; he would sin less!

Imagine if a husband understood that nothing could change the way his Father felt about him. Would he have to be depressed after a bad day at work or after getting fired, fearing he would be losing God's favor? Would he then have to take out his *fear* on his wife through anger or silence? No. His sin of anger and apathy would subside; he would sin less! And with less anger and apathy, he would love his wife more.

Imagine if the Truth in God's Word worked into our life. Truth as in Galatians and 1 John: "The person who lives in right relationship with God does it by embracing what God arranges for him. *Doing things for God is the opposite of entering into what God does for you.*"[59]

"*How did your new life begin? Was it by working your head off to please God?* Or was it by responding to God's Message to you? Are you going to continue this craziness?... Answer this question: Does the God who lavishly provides you with His own presence, His Holy Spirit, working things in your lives you could never do for yourselves—does He do these things because of your strenuous moral striving or because you trust Him to do them in you?"[60]

"God is love. When we take up permanent residence in a life of love, we live in God and God lives in us. This way, *love has the run of the house,* becomes at home, and matures in us....

There is no room in love for fear. Love banishes fear. Since fear is crippling, a fearful life is one not yet fully formed in love. We, though, are going to love—love and be loved. *First we were loved, now we love.* He loved us first."[61]

The Paradox of Performance

The paradoxical Truth about performance is that the more we focus on our performance, the worse it becomes. The more we try to attain perfection in one area, the more we allow our lives to unravel in others. The faster we run, the more we realize that we're chasing our own tail.

> The faster we run, the more we realize that we're chasing our own tail.

God doesn't want our performance to wane. He wants us *free* to perform. He wants us to be *free* to "take responsibility for doing the creative best we can with our own life."[62] But not through anxiety or stress-induced perfectionism that causes us to "choke up." Instead, through the freedom of knowing we are one of God's children. So we can relax, give it all we've got, and regardless of the outcome, we're going home to our Father's big hug tonight. So relax and make that free throw. Now that's freedom!

God Himself is our righteousness. God Himself is our goodness. Because of this miraculous transfer of His perfection to our imperfection, our actions are freed from the prison of performance. We are free!

THE FOUR STEPS & TEA

The key to breaking from the emotional prison of performance is summarized in four steps:

1. *Identify the unhealthy emotion.*
2. *Identify the unhealthy thought.*
3. *Identify the Truth.*
4. *Renew your mind.*

When you renew your mind through His timeless and infallible Truth, you will experience transformation from God in both your emotions and your behavior.

T: When your thoughts change, then…

E: your emotions will change, then…

A: your actions will change.

It is for freedom that Christ set us free. God designed us for freedom. Embrace His perfect plan and experience emotional and spiritual freedom through the renewal of your mind.

Additional Resources

Free "Four Step" worksheets are available from the downloads menu on the LivesTransforming.com website to guide you to freedom!

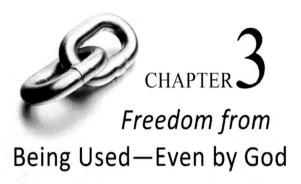

CHAPTER 3

Freedom from Being Used—Even by God

"We say, 'God intends me to be here because I am so useful!' God puts His saints where they will glorify Him, and we are no judges at all of where that is."
- Oswald Chambers

THE PRISON OF USEFULNESS
Disappointing

Linda's life was disappointing. She'd witnessed many Christians being used by God with great results. Her university, Anderson, was the proud home of many heavy hitters in the Christian world: Bill and Gloria Gaither, Sandi Patty, Steven Curtis Chapman, and a myriad of other people whose ministries have impacted the world. It was undeniable: God had used *them* to change the world. But what had *Linda* really done? How had *she* put herself in God's service, or, in the end, was she only a lukewarm servant? Did she ever "sell all she owned" or "drop her nets" to follow Christ? Or was she still clutching her own dreams and goals too tightly?

Linda was sure she knew the sad truth of it all. She had allowed herself to become too busy handling her own daily affairs—her secular job, the children, her marriage. But the guilt was always there under the surface. Linda felt with certainty that she wasn't *useful* to God. She was disappointing Him.

Never Doing Enough

Perhaps no greater anxiety exists in the minds of believers than a haunting sense that they are not being used by God. This relentlessly crushing burden is perhaps the worst kind of psychological prison because it is *pseudo-spiritual.*

We've all heard Christians (including ourselves) vent this nagging angst in all kinds of ways:

- "I'm not doing enough for God."
- "I don't really let God use me."
- "I haven't done my part to be useful to God."
- Or simply, "I'm useless!"

The toll this Prison of Usefulness is having on the Christian community is difficult to overstate. The Anxiety-Ridden Church Secretary. The Guilt-Laden Youth Minister. The Overbearing Prayer-Warrior Mom. There's always more to do, more ways to serve, more ways to be *useful.* Almost any direction you turn in Christian communities you encounter these Useful Addicts. And many of us find another addict when we look in the mirror.

Most of us have become so accustomed to this haunting voice of accusation that we simply do not recognize the full extent of the damage it is inflicting. But the truth is, this misconception is not simply a stumbling block to believers; it is downright crippling! Emotionally, psychologically, spiritually.

The emotional and psychological damage that arises from this potent sense of guilt has many faces. But generally people experience at least some level of depression or listlessness, which stems from a sense of defeat.

But far worse havoc can be wreaked by this lie. At its worst, this burden of "usefulness" can result in bouts of anxiety, social and professional withdrawal, or even a nervous breakdown.

Clearly, none of these emotional and psychological states appear in the descriptions of the fruit of the Spirit. In fact, it would be helpful to pause a moment and look again at the attributes of the Spirit as described by Paul in Galatians: "But the fruit of the Spirit is love, joy, peace, patience, kindness, goodness, faithfulness, gentleness, and self-control."[63]

The effects of believing yourself to be "useless" to God are always at odds with the Spirit living in in us. Love darkens to envy as we resent another's "more impactful" position. Joy diminishes under the weight of dejection and frustration. Peace is destroyed by unease and uncertainty.

This legacy of "rotten fruit" is clearly *not* the inheritance God has planned for us! But how do we break free from this pandemic? What exactly are the lies—and where do we find and apply the transformative Truths of God?

PRISON BREAK!
The Work of God

Our Father wants a relationship with us—not an employment contract! As with all psychological prisons, there is a sinister lie at the heart of the Prison of Usefulness.

The Truth is, God is not interested in *using* us. God is interested in *us*!

In the Gospel of Matthew, Christ says something that has the potential to shatter the cell walls of those who are in the prison of "usefulness."

"Are you tired? Worn out? Burned out on religion? Come to me. Get away with me and you'll recover your life. I'll show you how to take a real rest. Walk with me and work with me…watch how I do it. Learn the unforced rhythms of grace. I won't lay anything heavy or ill-fitting on you. Keep company with me and you'll learn to live freely and lightly."[64]

Peterson's translation of this famous direct quote of Christ tells us in comforting words what Christ offers us. Living "freely" and "lightly" in "unforced rhythms of grace" is music to the soul! It is the absolute antithesis of the guilt-ridden fear that we as Christians are not being "useful" enough. The relationship between us and God as described by Christ Himself does not contain even a hint of this foolish notion of usefulness.

Look closely. What exactly is Christ asking of us here? He says "come to me," "get away with me," "walk with me." In other words, he simply says, "Be with me." He assures us that he will not "lay anything heavy or ill-fitting" on us. Rather, he will teach us "to live freely and lightly."

So God wants me to "be with Him." But why? Do I serve a purpose to Him? Am I to be present as a maid or butler is present? Do I somehow benefit Him by "being with Him"?

In short, the answer is no. But let's look at a few more verses. The following oft-quoted passage from Psalm 139 has become an anthem for many Christians:

"For you created my inmost being; you knit me together in my mother's womb. I praise you because I am fearfully and wonderfully made; your works are wonderful, I know that full well."[65]

While this passage is batted back and forth in Christian circles, the extent of its power is often missed due to its familiarity.

The reality is this: God made *me* "fearfully and wonderfully"; I am *His* work and *all* His works are "wonderful"! Christ conveys this same transformative Truth in Luke 12:7: "And the very hairs on your head are all numbered. So don't be afraid; you are more valuable to Him than a whole flock of sparrows."[66]

God values us. We are valuable to God. Let that sink in—its depths are immeasurable. He knows it is hard for us to fathom, so He repeats it over and over in innumerable ways, like a patient and persistent wooing lover. In fact, the language of Christ in Matthew 11 *is* the language of love, a spiritual and holy courting of our souls.

We are valuable to God. Let that sink in.

Notice there is no caveat to God's proclamations of our worth. Christ does not insist that we *do* anything in particular for Him; all he asks is for us to trust in Him, to have faith in Him. God's high estimation of us does not involve our "use" to Him. No, God finds us inherently valuable—valuable because we are his dear creation, "fearfully and wonderfully made."

But doesn't our sinful behavior destroy the beauty of God's handiwork? Can't something be exquisitely made but fall into disrepair or be used for purposes for which it was never intended, thus losing its initial value?

Paul provides an answer to these questions in Romans: "Since we've compiled this long and sorry record as sinners (both us and them [New Testament Christians and Old Testament Jews]) and proved that we are utterly incapable of living the glorious lives God wills for us, God did it for us. *Out of sheer generosity He put us in right standing with Himself. A pure gift. He got us out of the mess we're in and restored us to where He always wanted us to be. And He did it by means of Jesus Christ.*"[67]

The "long and sorry list of sins" indeed *would be* a problem for us. But through Christ we are complete in Him and restored to our pristine condition.

"By entering through faith into what God has always wanted to do for us—set us right with Him, make us fit for Him—we have it all together with God because of our Master Jesus. And that's not all: We throw open our doors to God and discover at the same moment that He has already thrown open His door to us. We find ourselves standing where we always hoped we might stand—out in the wide open spaces of God's grace and glory, standing tall and shouting our praise."[68]

The Plunge into God!

In Oswald Chambers' masterful work, *If Thou Wilt Be Perfect: Talks on Spiritual Philosophy*, he addresses the issue of our value in God. He argues, as this book argues, that many of us do not involve our minds enough in our daily walk with Christ.

"Usually we leave our heads barren; we simply use our brains to explain our heart's experience."[69]

Chambers states that all of us believers know the deeper Truths of God in our spirit where God resides—that God's Truth is written within us. But too often, we do not *think* these Truths in our minds. The result? Our thought-life, our intellectual reality, is not taking full advantage of the freedom of Christ. One *particular* fact that we do not fully grasp with our minds is the reality of our own value. We fall for the world's lie: that our performance determines our value.

As Chambers says, "Do we really *think* what Jesus has taught us to know in our hearts, that apart from Him we can do nothing? We all believe it, but do we *think* it?"[70]

Our need for Christ to be in us is not something that arises in dire moments—it is a constant need. Outside of God, we are incompetent, completely "useless."

That is why we are to "be with Him" everywhere, all the time. We are not built to perform for Him; we are built to rely on Him. Our competence, our giftedness, our usefulness *is* Him. Thus we need Him; He doesn't need us.

This need is beautiful to God—it is His perfect and complete design. The more we embrace this reality, the more we will find ourselves at peace in the plan and work of God. Or as Chambers states, "We have to be so given over to God that we never think of our gifts [or talents or "usefulness"], then God can let His own life flow through us."[71]

Christ's call for us to come to Him and be with Him is a call to shed the self-prescribed chains of usefulness. We are to enter into His presence in a radical way, letting go of our anxiety-filled grip on our own performance and purpose. We are to take "an absolute plunge into the love of God!"[72]

> Christ's call for us to come to Him and be with Him is a call to shed the self-prescribed chains of usefulness.

The Living Water

The lie of the world is that we must focus vigilantly on being useful to God. The results of this futile pursuit are defeat, dejection, depression, and retreat.

Instead, we are called to renew our minds! We have been given the Truth in our hearts, so let us now allow those Truths transform our minds.

Chambers describes what a right perspective on our "usefulness" looks like: "The right attitude is to keep the mind absolutely concentrated on God and never get off on the line of how you are being *used* by Him."[73]

The common Christian obsession with being *used* actually

works against God's purpose for us. Instead, we must be "absorbed" in Him. Then out of us "will flow rivers of living water."[74] In the end, we should "have nothing to do with our *usability*, but only with our relationship to Jesus Christ; nothing must be allowed to come in between."[75] The paradoxical result of this profound Truth of God is nothing short of life transformation—the freedom to act *from within* God's purposes rather than incessantly trying to clean up after our human shortcomings.

The nature of our true design and the realization of our purpose in Christ wash away, with living water, the debilitating lie of being *used*. When we are *with* God, there is no question of what we are supposed to be *to* God. When we are *with* God, we find what He truly intends: a relationship with us!

A STORY OF LIBERATION
Does God *Use* His Children?

I met Linda in my conference room at work. After a short time of small talk, I could tell she was very sharp but also very "down." She was definitely an extrovert but also guarded. We had both gone to a Christian college together, Anderson University, and even after twenty years I could remember having deep conversations about God with her on campus. But after all those years a lot had changed. In college, we all had dreams of "the future" and what that would mean to our lives. After all, isn't that what college is all about—the future?

"Wow, it's been a long time," I started.

"Yeah, it sure has." Linda smiled through a frown.

"What's going on?"

"I wasn't sure who to even talk to about this, but someone told me to talk with you."

"Oh, boy, the pressure's on!" I laughed.

"I thought you went to school to become a Certified Public Accountant?"

"I did."

"Then why are you talking to people about—God and stuff?"

"CPAs aren't supposed to talk with people about God?"

"You know what I mean. Why are so many people coming to you to talk?"

"Actually, I don't know. I just try and meet with people when they call—simple as that."

"Hmmm."

"How about you, Linda?"

"I don't really use my college degree for anything. I guess, now that I think about it, maybe that's part of the issue."

"What issue is that?"

"I've really been struggling with depression."

"Is that what you want to talk about?"

"Yeah. I can't seem to beat it."

"So you've tried to overcome your depression but you can't?"

"That's right. And talking about college just makes it worse."

"What about college makes it worse?"

"All my life God has been an essential part of my life—and—" Linda started to cry. "And I haven't really given to Him."

"Given to Him—what do you mean?"

"Derek, you know. You went to Anderson University. It's the home of Bill and Gloria Gaither, Sandi Patty, Steven Curtis Chapman, and a myriad of other people whose ministries have impacted the world. God used them. I want to be able to make a difference, too. I just want God to use me, too."

"Let me make sure I understand. You are depressed because your Father isn't *using* you?"

"Yeah, I think so."

Linda's response was hesitant; she could tell by my tone that something was wrong with the word "using." And she was right.

"Using"—a word that we—uh—*use* all the time, a common one-syllable verb that we *employ* in diverse situations—so what's the problem with "use"?

All words carry with them the weight of all their potential interpretations, and the word "use" is no different. Use is a multifunctional word in English, one with subtle shifts in meaning depending on the context. It can mean simply *to put into service* ("use the tool"), but it can also mean *to use up* or *consume completely* ("use all the soap") and *to manipulate* ("use for personal gain"). While the first interpretation of *use* is rather neutral, the second two are loaded with meaning. The sense of "exhausting the supply" and "manipulating for personal gain" are inescapable connotations of "use."

I'm *Not* Supposed to Do Things for God?

I continued, "Linda, do you have children?"

"Yes. I have one son."

"How old is he?"

"He's seven years old."

"When was the last time you looked down at your son, grabbed his chin, and raised it up so he could see you. When was the last time you looked straight into his eyes and said, 'Son, I want to *use* you'?"

"That sounds a little gross, Derek...you're making me sound like a child molester or something."

"I agree. So why do you think your Father wants to *use* you?"

"I've never thought of it like that."

"Would you love your kids more if you could *use* them more?"

"No, that doesn't even make sense! I just like hanging out and being with my kids. They don't need to do anything for me."

"That's pretty normal, huh? Imagine having a Father who doesn't *need* anything from you, but instead, simply loves to hang out with you."

> "When was the last time you looked down at your son, grabbed his chin, and raised it up so he could see you. When was the last time you looked straight into his eyes and said, 'Son, I want to use you'?"

"I think I'd like that." Linda smiled.

"Me too."

"So are you saying that I'm not supposed to do anything for God?"

"Well, let's see. Do you do things with your kids?"

"Yes."

"So what makes you think that God doesn't want to do things *with* you?"

"I don't know. I've always thought of God as someone who expects me to do stuff *for* Him."

"Is there a difference between doing stuff *for Him* and doing stuff *with Him*?" I asked.

"Yes! A big difference. Believe me, my kids love doing stuff *with* me but it gets a little tougher when life is all about trying to get my kids to do stuff *for* me."

"That's why God is only interested in doing stuff *with* you."

"I don't understand…"

"Jesus put it this way: '*Live in me. Make your home in me just as I do in you.* In the same way that a branch can't bear grapes by itself but only by being joined to the vine, *you can't bear fruit unless you are joined <u>with</u> me.* I am the Vine, you are the branches. When you're joined <u>with</u> me and I <u>with</u> you, the relation intimate and organic, *the harvest is sure to be abundant.* Separated, you can't produce a thing. Anyone who separates from me is deadwood, gathered up and thrown on the bonfire. But if you make yourselves at home <u>with</u> me and my words are at home in you, you can be sure that whatever you ask will be listened to and acted upon. This is how my Father shows who he is—when you produce grapes, when you mature as my disciples.'"[76]

"Wow, that's amazing. That makes sense, but *how* do I do it. How do I join *with* God?"

Grafting

"The *how* is pretty simple really. Just open your eyes."

"What do you mean?"

"Did you ever see the movie *Joe Versus the Vo*lcano?"

"Was that a movie with Tom Hanks and Meg Ryan?"

"Yes."

"Yes, I thought it was pretty boring."

"Yeah, it was a little boring, but Patricia (played by Meg Ryan), in a moment out on a lake, made a comment I don't think I'll ever forget.

> "Only a few people are awake and they live in a state of constant total amazement."

She said, 'My father says that almost the whole world is asleep. Everybody you know. Everybody you see. Everybody you talk to. He says that *only a few people are awake* and they live in a state of constant total amazement.'"

"Derek, I don't understand. When you talk, I get totally lost. Eyes open—awake—I just don't get it."

"That's okay, Linda, it's really not about understanding; it's about it being revealed."

"See, there you go again."

"You're right; lots of people find me very—"

"Oh my gosh!"

"What?"

"This morning a neighbor came over and knocked on my door—"

"And—"

"She told me that she had baked some rolls for breakfast and she wanted to offer me some."

"That was nice of her—"

"No, Derek, you don't get it. She handed me the rolls and then mentioned that she'd like to get together and talk sometime. Derek, that was God, wasn't it? I see it now. But my eyes weren't open this morning. *That* was God wanting to join *with* me."

"Amazing, huh?"

"Yeah, but—"

"But what?"

"But is that really all there is to it?"

"What do you mean?"

"Well, look at the people we went to college with and how God—I don't know. Can having coffee with a neighbor really be important enough for God to join *with* me? Besides, don't you think that if I was 'good enough' God would give me something a little more important than a cup of coffee?"

Perfectly Useless

"So you think in order for God to join *with* you that it must be something important?"

"I don't know—I guess."

"Important to whom?"

"Hmmm. Yeah, I guess it really doesn't matter whether I think it's important. It matters whether God thinks it's important."

"Do you think God will want to join *with* you in something that is *not* important to Him?"

"No. But I guess it's easy to think that in order for it to be important to God, it must be recognized as important from the world's perspective. You know—Billy Graham, Bill Gaither, Rick Warren types."

"And that belief creates a strong feeling of—"

"Depression."

"It's so easy to pay attention to the world's perspective and not God's. From the world's perspective, we don't get picked for being *useless.*"

"Okay, now you're freaking me out again."

> "God places His saints where they will bring the most glory to Him, and we are totally incapable of judging where that may be."

I think Oswald Chambers summed it up best: "Look at God's incredible waste of His saints, according to the world's judgment. God seems to plant His saints in the most useless places. And then we say, 'God intends for me to be here because I am so useful to Him.' Yet Jesus never measured His life by how or where He was of the greatest use. God places His saints where they will bring the most glory to Him, and we are totally incapable of judging where that may be."[77]

THE PARADOX OF USEFULNESS

God created us in a very special, creative, and gifted way. Every single one of us has a list of gifts, talents, resources, and special abilities that not only empowers us as individuals but also enhances the lives of those around us. However, God did not create us to compare our gifts and talents with those around us or to obsess over who is "more useful" or more effective for His Kingdom. These are the futile equations of the world. Christ died for the sins of those who would accept Him, opening up a real relationship with God and offering the eternal inheritance of children of God. He freed us from the lies that our value is based on anything but God.

Let's look again at the salvation statement presented earlier.

Salvation Statement

- I am a new creation of infinite worth.
- I am completely forgiven.
- I am fully pleasing to God.
- I am totally accepted by God.
- And I am absolutely complete.
- I am righteous.
- I am completely loved; there is nothing I can do or say that will make God love me more and nothing I can do to make God love me less.
- I am what God says I am. This is God's Truth, and God's Truth is unchanging, incorruptible, indestructible…it is the ever living Word of God.

The perfection and completion of Christ's work on the Cross has completed and perfected *us*. We are "fully pleasing" to God, "totally accepted," unable to make ourselves more or less valuable based on our "usefulness" to Him through anything we do.

It is not our calling *to be used* by Him. It is this sort of thinking that leads to a performance-based perspective of ourselves. This ultimately divisive and debilitating perspective often leads to the very opposite of the intended results. Defeat, dejection, depression, retreat. Everything counter to the fruit of the Spirit. Certainly this is not God's purpose for us.

> When we are free from the need to be used by God, something amazing happens.

So what is our true calling? God calls us all to *draw near* to Him, *walk alongside* Him, *be with* Him.

When we are free from the need to be used by God, something amazing happens. We connect with our Father in a relationship. And in the living out of that relationship, we join God in our daily life, and guess what? Then, and only then, the Kingdom is advanced (and this is the True definition of "being used")!

THE FOUR STEPS & TEA

To sum up, the key to breaking from the emotional prison of thinking we must be used by God is summarized in four steps:

1. *Identify the unhealthy emotion.*
2. *Identify the unhealthy thought.*
3. *Identify the Truth.*
4. *Renew your mind.*

When you renew your mind through His timeless and infallible Truth, you will experience transformation from God in both your emotions and your behavior:

T: When your thoughts change, then…

E: your emotions will change, then…

A: your actions will change.

It is for freedom that Christ set us free. God designed us for freedom. Embrace His perfect plan and experience the emotional and spiritual freedom through the renewal of your mind.

Additional Resources

Free "Four Step" worksheets are available from the downloads menu on the LivesTransforming.com website to guide you to freedom!

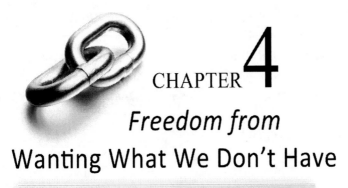

CHAPTER 4

Freedom from
Wanting What We Don't Have

> *"He had discovered a great law of human action, without knowing it—namely, in order to make a man or boy covet a thing, it is only necessary to make the thing difficult to attain."*
> - Mark Twain

THE PRISON OF WANTS

"Want" Tyranny

As you'll see, the three individuals below—Sally, Gary, and Ray—though they are all in different situations, are all caught up in the tyranny of wanting.

All Sally wanted was a healthy relationship with her father. Was that too much to ask? Isn't that a good thing to want? A functional father-daughter relationship—what could be wrong with that? But the more she tried to create it, the more out of reach it seemed. She was frustrated and sad. Why wasn't God blessing her noble efforts to mend the relationship?

Gary, on the other hand, had become something he'd always hated. He'd become the classic controlling husband. His wife complained about his domineering behavior. His friends agreed with his wife. He had become—a jerk. And it was wrecking his family. How had this happened? All he was trying to do was encourage his wife to make him a priority. He was tired of being third or fourth on her list. Wasn't it her biblical duty to put him first?

He wasn't happy and neither was she. And he was becoming increasingly frustrated and confused. Why couldn't he make his wife understand?

Ray was also in a bad place. He called it a "rut," but to be honest it was far deeper than that. His wife had recently left him and his daughter was pulling away more every day. Ray felt like all the blessings of his life were being withdrawn one by one. If only he could get it all back! Get back his daughter, win back his wife! If he could just do what he needed to do to get his family back, he could be happy again. But nothing seemed to be working.

The Oldest Lie in the Book

Not to be overdramatic, but this emotional prison may be based on the oldest and most prevalent lie in the universe. What was Adam and Eve's problem? You often hear that it was a lack of faith or trust in God's goodness. However, there's another angle that too often goes unrecognized. Coveting. Wanting what they did not have. Wasn't the major lie from the Enemy a lie of "wants"—a sales job, a deceptively appealing false need?

The coveting lie may be the most foundational lie known to mankind. The best definition that I have found for coveting is: *I want what I don't have or I want to be who I'm not!*

As God's Word shows, and history shows, and our lives prove every day, this prison is treacherous. Wanting what we do not have is a tyrannical master. Adam and Eve, Cane and Abel, the Israelites and the golden calf—the Old Testament is crowded with cautionary tales about this lie of lies.

Wanting what we do not have is a tyrannical master.

We see the obvious tyranny of worldly wants all around us: the greed for money devouring a person's moral fiber; the obsession with fame leading to increasingly self-destructive behavior; the desire for status consuming one's spiritual foundation. The *obvious* "tyranny of wants" is easy to decry—and thus, for many Christians, relatively easy to avoid. But what about the *subtle* tyrannies?

I've found that many Christians are too savvy to fall for the Big Three Lies: money, fame, and success. We've read and reread the Bible's cautionary tales; we've heard sermon after sermon reaffirming the undesirability of these false desires. But what about the wants that go under the radar? Here are two questions to get your mind going.

Question 1: What are three things *you want but don't have*?

Think about it—even better, write down the results. I asked this question of a group I led and here were a few of the results:

- I want my kids to do chores cheerfully.
- I want blonde hair (without the chemicals).
- I want financial freedom.
- I want to be responsible.
- I want my husband to be responsible.
- I want to be irresponsible.
- And my favorite…I want a do-over!

What is striking about these "wants" is how reasonable they are. These are the kind of desires we can all relate to—likely the kind we're experiencing in some measure right now. They are not particularly selfish (except perhaps numbers 2 and 6); in fact, a few of them could be considered markedly *unselfish*. Wanting to be responsible, wanting one's children to learn the importance of contributing to the household, simply wanting to be free of financial burdens (perhaps to be able to give more to one's church or charities). What could be wrong with such wants? Hold that thought, and consider another question.

> Wanting to be responsible, wanting one's children to learn the importance of contributing to the household, simply wanting to be free of financial burdens. What could be wrong with such wants?

Question 2: What is one thing that *you want to be that you are not?*

A few common answers from Christians:

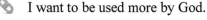
- I want to be more influential.
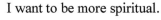
- I want to be more spiritual.
- I want to be used more by God.

Again, notice the reasonableness of these wants. Being "more influential" offers more opportunity for service and impact. Being "more spiritual" certainly can't be wrong, right? Aren't these *good* wants...?

The Enemy Loses the Battle to Win the War

If you have been a Christian for a while or if you have been around church much, it is highly likely your list does *not* include the flagrant or blatantly "bad wants"—things like "I want to be filthy rich" or "I want to be famous." Why? Here are two possible reasons:

1. Somewhere along the line it has been communicated to you that fame and fortune don't satisfy. Maybe you've even read Ecclesiastes and in the back of your mind you think...I shouldn't want "those things."

2. Another reason we don't write "I want fame and fortune" is because, although we do *want* them, people would probably think we were being vain if we admitted that *out loud.* So we keep it a secret.

So the Enemy lets us win the little battle of the blatantly bad wants, and instead, he goes after us in a very different way.

Instead of firing an arrow at your head that says, *"You should want fame and fortune"*—a battle he knows he may not win—he fires off another arrow, one more likely to be effective. It goes something like this:

"You should want to be more influential."

"You should want to be more spiritual."

"You should want your friends to come to Christ."

Or more specifically from the stories above:

"You should want your wife to treat you with respect."

"You should want to win your family back."

"You should want a healthy relationship with your dad."

These are all good things. In fact, they're deceptively good. The Enemy often doesn't shoot arrows from "high angles" (the obviously tyrannical desires)—he aims at our

> The Enemy often doesn't shoot arrows from "high angles"— he aims at our feet, attempting to trip us up.

feet, attempting to trip us up. He attempts to twist even these "good wants" into a mangled, entangling mess.

PRISON BREAK!

"I Want a Healthy Relationship with My Dad"

A simple, seemingly healthy thought like: "I want a healthy relationship with my dad." How can that thought possibly trip us up? How can that be unhealthy? Is it possible it could even be based on a lie? Ouch—as my daughter would say, "You're going to have to show me that in the Bible."

First, how do we know if this thought is a lie? Simple—many of you know already. Ask yourself what emotions are associated with the thought. This is how you take your spiritual temperature. When you think a thought...what do you feel? Do you feel peace and joy—the fruit of the Spirit? That's how you tell if it's based on a lie or not. It was pretty easy for Sally to decide it was based on a lie. Here are her notes.

Sally's Notes

Step 1. **What are the unhealthy, "unfruitful" emotions?**
   "Anger, frustration, and tears."

Step 2. **What is the thought that led to those emotions?**
   "I want a healthy relationship with my dad."

What are the lies at the heart of that thought?

> "I want something I don't have."

> "I want a healthy relationship with my dad because it makes me feel bad when he doesn't like me."

> "Because of my relationship with my dad, there must be something wrong with me. I feel like I'm somehow 'less' than what I should be."

Step 3. What is the Truth?

"I already have everything I need in me, because God is in me, and that is what makes my life valuable and complete. My life is already complete."[78]

"My dad's opinion of me can never change my worth or value as a person. I don't need a relationship with my dad to feel better about myself."[79]

"God in me has already made me righteous (good enough for even God), and nothing can change that!"[80]

"I don't have to have a tyrannical need for a relationship with my dad anymore. I'll be just fine." *(Wow, what a relief!)*

Step 4. Now that I know the Truth—Renew! Renew! Renew!

Sally had been living her life based on a lie.
The Old Thought (T):
"I want a healthy relationship with my dad."
The Old Emotions (E):
Anger, frustration, and tears.
The Old Actions (A):
A nasty letter, verbal arguments, and fights with her dad.
But when Sally recognized the freedom offered her through God's Word, she could see what her life could look like.
The New Thought (T):
"I love my dad. But a healthy relationship with my dad doesn't impact who I am or how I feel about myself. I love him, but I don't need him to love me."
The New Emotions (E):

Relief, peace, and empathy.

The New Actions (A):

A letter. One that tells her dad that she loves him. However, she understands that he may not want a relationship with her, and that is okay.

Which scenario, living in the lie or living in the Truth,  creates a more likely situation for reconciliation? While there's never a guarantee in this life that people will respond rightly to someone else's right actions, the answer is clear: Sally is far more likely to find reconciliation with her father when she allows God's Truth to permeate her life and doesn't need (covet) the relationship.

The Freedom of God's Sufficiency

Regardless of how the reconciliation with her father turns out, Sally will be able to experience the freedom of God's sufficiency in this area of her life. The coveting lie and the resultant tyranny of wants is literally the oldest trick in the Book, but the Truth is there from the beginning as well. "In the beginning God..."[81] When He is *our* beginning and end, our sole desire, we will experience freedom like we've never known it.

I think Peter said it best: "Since Jesus went through everything I'm going through and more, I'm learning to think like Him. I think of my sufferings as a weaning from that old sinful habit of always expecting to *get my way*. Then I'm able to live out my days *free* to pursue what God wants instead of being *tyrannized* by what I want."[82]

STORIES OF LIBERATION
"When Family Priorities Ruin Your Marriage"
You Want Me to Want Her to Sin?

I was having a late breakfast with Gary. He got right to the point. "Derek, I just can't get over the frustration and anger I feel in my marriage. Things aren't going well and I'm at my wits' end. I don't think our marriage is going to last."

"You're frustrated."

"Yeah, and I'm stuck," said Gary.

"Do you know why you're frustrated?"

"I just think family priorities are an important thing."

"How is thinking that family priorities are important frustrating you?"

"I just want my wife to make me a priority. Right now it's kids first, then work, then Facebook, then maybe me."

"So you are saying that you are frustrated because you want your wife to make you a priority?"

"Yeah, is that so bad?"

"No, that's good!" I said.

"What do you mean?"

"I mean it's awesome that you know what is causing your frustration."

"Why is that awesome?" Gary asked with a touch of skepticism.

"Because if you know what is frustrating you, then you know how to get rid of it!"

"I don't understand."

"Okay, for example, one time my son broke out in hives and started having problems breathing. We rushed him to the doctor and they immediately stuck an IV in his arm and started pumping Benadryl into him. He was having a horrible allergic reaction, and frankly, if we hadn't reached the emergency room on time, he would have died."

"What happened?"

"Something awesome happened. We found out that Connor was deathly allergic to walnuts. So let me ask you something—if walnuts were killing my son, what is the cure?"

"Not eating walnuts."

"That's right! It's awesome to know what was killing my son, because now we know how to save his life."

"Derek, can I be honest with you?"

"Sure."

"I'm sympathetic to your kid and all, but what in the world does this story have to do with my marriage?"

"Well, now that you know what's causing your frustration and anger with your marriage, then—"

"Then what?" he asked, this time with a touch of irritation.

"Okay, let's start again. If the thought 'I want my wife to make me a priority' is causing you to be angry, then what will eliminate the frustration and anger?"

"Are you saying I should *not* want my wife to make me a priority? You want me to *want* her to sin? Are you nuts?"

"No, I'm not asking you to want her to sin. I'm asking you whether your anger would decrease if you didn't *need* your wife to do what you wanted her to do in order for you to be happy with your marriage."

"Geesh, say that again," he said, shaking his head.

"Gary, would your anger decrease if you didn't *need* your wife to make you a priority?"

"Yeah, I guess so."

"Would you have to be frustrated with your marriage?"

"So you want me to just let her get by with putting me low on the totem pole even though the Bible—"

"What is your alternative?"

"My alternative is to *not* let her get by with it."

"You mean you want me to give you some sort of biblical permission to control and manipulate your wife into doing what you want her to do so you'll feel better about yourself and your marriage?"

Silence.

It seemed I had struck a chord in Gary—one of those moments we've all experienced where the

Would your anger decrease if you didn't need your wife to make you a priority?

advice and comments of others over time all converge to a point. But something else was going on inside Gary—the struggle to understand biblical hierarchies of Truth. Does one of God's commandments ever override another? While the answer is an emphatic *no*, many times believers are left confused by apparent contradictory commands—as Gary was about to point out.

Gross

Gary sat staring at nothing for what seemed like an hour. Finally, he broke the silence.

"My wife tells me I'm controlling. Derek, I don't know what to do, but I think it's ripping our relationship apart. I get so confused about what the Bible is saying!"

"I understand. Gary, remember, the Enemy has an incredible talent for deceiving all of us. But let's try something."

"Okay."

"Give me just one benefit of you *not* needing your wife to make you a priority."

"Derek, I don't *need* her to make me a priority. I just *want* her to make me a priority."

"So your happiness with your marriage isn't connected to your wife making you a priority?"

"Well, actually my happiness *is* connected to her making me a priority."

"Then you *need* her! Anytime our emotional health and well-being are *dependent* on another person, it's a *need*, not a *want*."

"Okay, I see that now. Let's start again."

"Okay, give me just one benefit of you *not* needing your wife to make you a priority."

"That's easy. If I didn't need her to make me a priority, then I wouldn't be so frustrated and angry with her all the time."

> Anytime our emotional health and well-being is dependent on another person, it's a need not a want.

"Great! That's exactly right."

"Give me another benefit of you *not* needing your wife to make you a priority."

"I can't think of any."

"Does your need to have your wife make you a priority help your marriage?"

"It will help our marriage *if* she makes me a priority!" Gary replied, continuing to confuse himself.

"No, that's not what I mean. Imagine you are back in college when you and Lindsay were dating."

"Okay."

"Now imagine you go up to her and tell her how desperately you *need* her to make you a priority in her life. How you can't live without her. Without her, your life would have no meaning and you'd be depressed, frustrated, and angry for the rest of your life."

"That would be gross!"

"Would it endear her to you?"

"No, it would probably gross her out, push her away. I would have never said anything like that. That would guarantee she wouldn't want to be around me."

"So why are you communicating this same message to your wife now?"

"Oh, I never thought of it like that before."

"So now give me another benefit to *not* needing your wife to make you a priority."

"I won't gross my wife out! It might actually endear her to me rather than repel her away from me."

"Great. I agree. And as you make connections with your wife in a way that endears her to you, will she want to be around you more or less?"

"Chances are she'd want to be around me more. Not less. Okay, okay, okay. I'm starting to see this, but it sounds like you are saying that me wanting my wife to put me first is somehow wrong or sinful. I want to know where this stuff is in the Bible!"

The Original Sin

"It all started in Genesis," I said. "I believe it's Satan's most potent weapon. Watch how Satan shot this lie at Eve....

"The serpent told the Woman, 'You won't die. God knows that the moment you eat from that tree, you'll see what's really going on. You'll be just like God, knowing everything, ranging all the way from good to evil.' *(You will get what you don't have!)* When the Woman saw that the tree looked like good eating and realized what she would get out of it—she'd know everything!—*(she wanted what she didn't have)* she took and ate the fruit and then gave some to her husband, and he ate."[83]

I continued, "The Enemy didn't deceive Adam and Eve by threatening them. He deceived them by convincing them that if they could get something 'good' that they didn't already have, then their life would be better."

"So that's what coveting is, isn't it?" Gary realized.

"Yes, it's the Original Sin. Satan deceived Eve by convincing her that she should *want* what she didn't have."

> Satan deceived Eve by convincing her that she should want what she didn't have.

"And I *want* what I don't have. I *want* my wife to make me a priority."

"Yep, and the lie of coveting will always lead to the 'deeds of the flesh,' like unhealthy anger, rage, strife, depression, etc.[84] The Enemy exists with a purpose to destroy you and your marriage, and this is one of his favorite tools of the trade. He even tried it on Jesus."

"How so?"

"Remember when Satan was in the garden tempting Jesus? For the second test, he (Satan) led Him (Jesus) up and spread out all the kingdoms of the earth on display at once. Then the Devil said, 'They're yours in all their splendor to serve your pleasure. (*You can get what you don't have...It's all good stuff too!*) I'm in charge of them all, and I can turn them over to whomever I wish. Worship me and they're yours; the whole works.'

"Jesus refused, again backing His refusal with Deuteronomy: 'Worship the Lord your God and only the Lord your God. Serve Him with absolute single-heartedness.' (*I don't want what I don't have. I have all I need already: God!*)."[85]

"I see it now," Gary replied. "Wanting my wife to make me a priority in order for me to feel good about my marriage is—"

"Anytime you *want* what you don't have and your emotional health or happiness depends on it—even when it's a good thing, like family, financial stability, or the salvation of a friend—you know you are coveting. And the Enemy will use this lie to seek and destroy your life from the inside out."

"I Want My Family Back."
The Rut

When Ray came to see me, he looked defeated.

"Derek, I don't think I'll ever get out of this rut I'm in. I see no way out."

"Rut? I don't know what you mean."

"It's like Groundhog Day every day of my life," replied Ray, with eyes half open.

"So every day is the same?"

"Yep, ever since my wife left me, it's been the same day over and over again."

"Are you saying that you don't like the rut you are in?"

"*Hello*, genius boy...I think you're catching on!" Ray responded sarcastically. "I hate this rut I'm in. Every day's the same—I come home from work to a lonely house and watch the clock tick away until I see my daughter again."

> "I come home from work to a lonely house and watch the clock tick away until I see my daughter again."

"Actually, I think there are advantages to the rut you are living in."

"Are you crazy? Man, sometimes I think you're nuts!"

"No, really. Your rut could have a number of advantages."

"Come on, Derek. I really don't want to talk about it." Ray shook his head and rolled his eyes.

"Okay, maybe you're right. Maybe you *do* want to move on."

"Huh?" Fear and curiosity showed on his face.

"You were arguing there were no advantages to being in a rut. If there are no advantages, that must mean you are ready to move on."

Ray leaned heavily on the counter and stared at me for a long time. "I—I—I don't know." The deeper issue was surfacing. A tear rolled down his cheek and splashed onto the countertop.

"What don't you know, Ray?"

"I don't know if I'm ready to move on."

"Why?"

The Way It Was

"Moving on" is a weighty concept in many Christians' lives. The internal conflict between our natural resistance to letting go of the past—with all its attendant memories, habits, desires, and *needs*—and our rational knowledge about the need to let go and move into a new phase is sometimes a brutal contest.

Paul's assertion that he strives to be "forgetting what is behind and straining toward what is ahead"[86] is pitted against our desire to control our lives by keeping hold of the past. Often we let our desires overthrow God's Word.

Ray was going through the battle right before my eyes.

"Derek, I don't like my life right now. I liked my life the way it was. I had a wife and a daughter—"

"And if you move on, then—"

"Then I'd be giving all that up. I'd be giving up the very thing that gave me so much happiness for so many years. I liked my life the way it was. How can I give up something that was so good? God blessed me with a wife and a daughter, and it's all gone."

"It doesn't sound like it's gone."

"What do you mean?"

"It sounds like the life you used to have is very real to you. It sounds like you are living in it every day."

"It's an old friend, and I can't stand the thought of it going away."

"There is quite an advantage to your rut, huh?"

"Yes, now I see it. If I get out of my rut, it's like I've lost an old friend. I'd have to lose what is most dear to me. I'd have to give

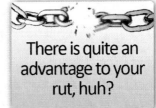

There is quite an advantage to your rut, huh?

up my wife and daughter. I'd have to give up on the best years of my life. How can God want me to give up such a good thing?"

"You mentioned earlier that you hated living in a rut."

"I do hate living in a rut, but 'moving on' is unfathomable. I feel like I'd just be giving up."

"So what are your options?"

"I don't know. I just want my family back! Is that such a bad thing?"

"That's what will make you happy?"

"Yes."

"Have you tried to get your family back?"

"Yes, I've tried everything."

"So you've tried hard to get what *you* want?"

"You are starting to make it sound like wanting my family back is bad. God wants families to stay together, Derek. This is not about what *I* want; this is about what *God* wants!"

"I'm not saying God doesn't want families to stay together; I'm just curious whether it has worked?"

"What do you mean?"

"Has it worked to try and get what you (and God) want?"

"No. It seems like the harder I try, the worse it gets."

"What do you mean?"

"Well, my wife won't even return my calls now, and my

daughter seems distant."

"So trying to get what you want isn't working."

"No."

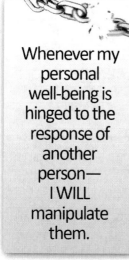

Whenever my personal well-being is hinged to the response of another person— I WILL manipulate them.

"How do you think your wife feels when you continue to try and get her to do what you (and God) want her to do?"

"She probably feels like I'm trying to control her," Ray replied heavily.

"A friend once told me, *'Whenever my personal well-being is hinged to the response of another person—I WILL manipulate them.'* So trying to get your wife to do what you want so you will be happy—"

"Leads to manipulation and control."

"Absolutely!"

"But now I'm more confused than ever!"

The Tyranny

"So I'm NOT supposed to care about my wife and daughter anymore?" Ray was confused about what to feel at this point. The Enemy had tied the Truth up in knots.

"Ray, are you saying that getting what YOU want is the same thing as caring about your wife and daughter?"

"No," Ray sighed. "I guess not."

"In fact, the more you focus on getting what you want—"

"The more I try to manipulate her, the *less* I'm caring about my wife and the *more* I'm caring about *me*."

"Okay. So that's what it does to *her*—but what does it do to *you*?"

"It makes my life miserable. It's a horrible way to live, but I still don't understand. Why does God want me to give up something that is so good, like my wife?"

"Ray, giving up the bad stuff can be pretty easy, in some obvious ways. Alcohol gives you a hangover, drugs cause withdrawal, and cheap sex leaves you empty. But giving up the 'good stuff,' things like a good job, a thriving ministry, or a family, can be far more difficult but just as important. You see, *the things we treasure in life are the most important to give up.* Or as Oswald Chambers states, 'Don't be deceived into believing that mammon is to be associated with only sordid things.'"[87]

"I don't understand."

"We all know how ridiculous it is to connect our happiness to something like alcohol, right?"

"Yes."

"Well, when the Enemy can't tempt you with something like alcohol anymore, he'll change tactics. He'll tempt you by trying to make you believe you need the 'good stuff' to complete your life. *But the Truth is that nothing OUTSIDE of yourself completes you.*"[88]

The truth is that nothing OUTSIDE of yourself completes you.

Gary was silent.

"It's exactly what the Enemy did when he was with Jesus in the desert. He tempted Jesus by telling Him he could have food (turn the stone into bread) and a good job (overseeing the kingdoms of the earth). It seems like food and a good job would be things God would want us to have.[89] After all, most of us would think of those temptations as 'blessings' from God, wouldn't we?" I asked.

Gary's eyes were now wide open. "I've never looked at it like that, but I see what you mean. When I want the 'good stuff,' it tyrannizes my life just as much as the 'bad stuff.'"

"Exactly."

"Where is this stuff in the Bible?"

"Here it is...'Since Jesus went through everything you're going through and more; *learn to think like Him.* Think of your sufferings (losing your family) as a weaning from that old sinful habit of always expecting to get your own way. Then you'll be able to live out your days *free* to pursue what God wants instead of *being tyrannized* by what you want.'"[90]

"My Needs and Your Needs..."

I've heard comments like this a million times—okay, maybe not a million—how about you?

She Thinks...

If he would just show a little affection—is that too much to ask?

(He <u>should</u> show more affection.)

With the job he has, I never know for sure where the next paycheck is coming from—is a little stability too much to ask?

(I <u>should</u> have more stability.)

A little conversation would be nice. All I'm asking for is some meaningful conversation.

(He <u>should</u> communicate.)

He never opens up! If he would just be honest, THEN maybe we'd be fine.

(He <u>should</u> be open and honest.)

He works all the time. Don't you think a father should set aside a little time to be with his kids?

(He <u>should</u> be a better dad.)

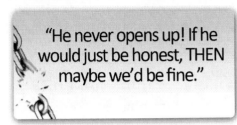

"He never opens up! If he would just be honest, THEN maybe we'd be fine."

He Thinks...

If she would just pick up—the house is such a mess. I'm embarrassed to invite people over, never mind feeling comfortable there myself!
(She <u>should</u> be more responsible.)

It's been weeks, and she NEVER initiates! Come on, it's out of control.
(She <u>should</u> initiate in the bedroom.)

I'm not asking for a beauty queen but she doesn't even try.
(She <u>should</u> take better care of herself.)

Nothing I do is good enough. I work my butt off and she doesn't appreciate anything.
(She <u>should</u> appreciate me.)

"Nothing I do is good enough. I work my butt off and she doesn't appreciate anything."

She never wants to do anything fun; she doesn't like anything I like. A little selflessness would go a long way. (She <u>should</u> be willing to do at least some of the things I enjoy.)

Have you ever had thoughts like these? Have you ever heard other people make these comments? I thought so—me too! Satan loves pulling these arrows (lies) out of his quiver on a daily basis and letting them fly.

Dangerous Christian Marriage Counseling

There is an *entire* industry out there trying to tell you how to fix your marriage and here's the kind of advice that is offered:

You need to figure out what HER needs are and then you SHOULD meet them.

You need to figure out what HIS needs are and then you SHOULD meet them.

And if you do *that*, you will live happily, happily, happily ever after!

It's *not* that attempting to understand the differences between men and women and the way we are naturally wired is a "bad thing." In fact, these marriage courses are being taught all over the nation in churches. *You* may actually be taking one or teaching one right now! Honestly, I recommended these books and resources for years.

Participants would get all excited. They would see the light at the end of the tunnel and start to imagine eternal marital bliss just around the corner.

And then—lurking around the corner, the Enemy fires his arrow. "Come on, you *deserve* to have your needs met, to get your spouse to change, to get what you want."

A Few Months Later

After teaching one of these courses or recommending a book with the thesis that "your spouse *should* meet your needs if you are going to have a happy marriage," I would end up having a conversation like this…

"How are you doing, Sue?"

"Oh, pretty good I guess, but things have been a little rough at home lately."

"Really? I thought after that marriage course, things were really moving in the right direction."

"They are—I mean they were—I mean I thought they were."

"What happened?"

"Well, I really learned a lot and I followed the program to the 'T.' I did everything I could to meet my husband's needs."

"And?"

"Derek, do you know what it's like to do everything possible for your spouse and get nothing in return? I don't know how much longer I can handle this marriage. I've done everything I know how to do! But am I supposed to just give, give, and give?"

Statistical Proof

Who has a better chance of staying married, Christians or atheists? The answer is revealing.

The Barna Research Group, an evangelical Christian organization that does surveys and research to better understand what Christians believe and how they behave, studied divorce rates in America.[91]

> When we "should" all over our spouses the Enemy drives a wedge deep between us.

It's hard to believe, but they "found surprising evidence that divorce is far lower among atheists than among conservative

Christians—exactly the opposite of what they were probably expecting."[92]

Unbelievable! Well, not really. Think about it. With all these expectations of what your wife "should do" and your husband "should do" so you can be happy in your marriage, is it any wonder that satisfaction in marriage is hard to find? When we rain "shoulds" all over our spouses, the Enemy drives a wedge deep between us. This is one of the Enemy's greatest tactics to use against Christians! Ask yourself:

- *Do these thoughts help?*
- *Does it make the other person change?*
- *Does it help me feel better?*
- *Does it solve my problems?*

The answer, of course, is NO, NO, NO, and NO! Wanting what we don't have (coveting) is a heat-seeking missile aimed at our relationships with an intent to destroy our marriages.

THE PARADOX OF WANTS

The coveting lie and the resultant tyranny of wants is literally the oldest trick in the Book. But the Good Book also tells us in all kinds of ways, from all kinds of angles, what the one truly *good* want is: God Himself.

> When the coveting lie is replaced by the Truth of God's all-sufficiency in our life, we are free to pursue God!

You should desire God "with all your heart, and with all your soul, and with all your mind, and with all your strength."[93]

We should "want" God with *all* of ourselves. "As the deer pants for streams of water, so my soul pants for you, O God."[94] There should be nothing left in us "wanting." God is the satisfaction of *all* our needs for *all* circumstances and in *all* situations.

122

When the coveting lie is replaced by the Truth of God's all-sufficiency in our life, we are free to pursue God! Freedom from wanting what we don't have or wanting to be who we are not allows us to fully participate in God's blessing. We are like Jesus, learning to live entirely dependent on God.[95]

The paradoxical result is that by focusing on God's sufficiency, we actually get the happiness and contentment we thought the things we wanted to have or wanted to be would get us. Again and again, God reminds us of this. Our part is to repeat His timeless words. Let's review this verse one more time...

"Since Jesus went through everything I'm going through and more, I'm learning to think like Him. I think of my sufferings as a weaning from that old sinful habit of always expecting to *get my way*. Then I'm able to live out my days *free* to pursue what God wants instead of being *tyrannized by what I want.*"[96]

THE FOUR STEPS & TEA

To sum up, the key to breaking from the emotional prison of wanting what we don't have is summarized in four steps:

1. *Identify the unhealthy emotion.*
2. *Identify the unhealthy thought.*
3. *Identify the Truth.*
4. *Renew your mind.*

When you renew your mind through His timeless and infallible Truth, you will experience transformation from God in both your emotions and your behavior.

T: When your thoughts change, then...

E: your emotions will change, then...

A: your actions will change.

It is for freedom that Christ set us free. God designed us for freedom. Embrace His perfect plan and experience the emotional and spiritual freedom through the renewal of your mind.

Additional Resources

Free "Four Step" worksheets are available from the downloads menu on the LivesTransforming.com website to guide you to freedom!

CHAPTER 5

Freedom from the Past and Future

> *"We long for some thing that is not and shut our eyes to the thing that is... this craving to go somewhere else, to see the things that are distant, arises from a refusal to attend to what is near (God!)."*
> - Oswald Chambers

THE PRISON OF THE FUTURE
Imprisoning Predictions

Our daily lives are plagued with predictions. Recognize any of these?

- *I'm going to get fired.*
- *She's going to hate me.*
- *I'm going to flunk the test.*

- *He's never going to learn.*
- *What if he leaves me?*
- *What if the plane is late?*
- *What if she changes her mind?*
- *What if we go bankrupt?*
- *What if I never get that vacation, or car, or house, or promotion, or, or, or, or, or—*

If you've never had thoughts like these, you are probably—well—not breathing! Satan loves pulling these arrows (lies) out of his quiver on a daily basis and letting them fly toward as many people as possible. Soon we end up looking like St. Sebastian, riddled with anxiety-inducing arrows.

While each of these worrisome questions has its own nuances of deception, all of them are connected by one foundational lie.

Look closely and you'll see it. All these lies are based on anxiety-inducing predictions of the future. But let's get more specific....

My Trip to Denver

I woke up at 4:00 A.M. Tuesday in a stupor and headed out the door to the airport. It was 28 degrees and it wasn't supposed to start raining until later that day. I got a seat inside the terminal about an hour before takeoff. (An hour? Yes, I was with my dad—ex military—you get the picture.)

Anyway, I'm watching the planes take off without a hitch. Then it's time to board the plane. The plane pulls away from the concourse and starts to taxi toward liftoff, then stops. It has started to rain—freezing rain—so the de-icer trucks pull up and spray a blanket of mist over the top of us. The plane again starts to taxi down the runway and again comes to a stop. The pilot announces that ice pellets are starting to fall, and since the de-icing fluid does not work with ice pellets, he would "be in touch."

I called a friend of mine on my cell and was told the freezing rain was forecast to last for another five hours. Hmmm—this could be a while. So I turned on my iPod and started listening to Gershwin's "Rhapsody in Blue" (appropriate for an airline flight, yes?). BUT within a few minutes, the loudspeaker came on again; it was the pilot, announcing that we'd been cleared for takeoff.

Whoa, I thought. *Wait just a minute!* The pilot just told us we had to wait for the weather to change because of the ice pellets. Was I supposed to believe that suddenly that no longer applied? The ice pellets were still falling!

Then the arrow was aimed and fired right at me: *What if the plane goes down during takeoff?*

Anxiety shot through my body (like an arrow), sending a chill down my spine. My stomach churned.

—Score one for the Enemy!

The Crystal Ball Lie

Obviously, I didn't know what was *really* going to happen, but the Enemy attacked with, "Hey, Derek, let's start thinking about what *might* happen." He was attempting to get me to believe in one of his favorite lies...

"You <u>can</u> predict the future."

Now if I asked you point blank, "Can you predict the future?" you would say, "Of course not!" But that doesn't stop the Enemy from shooting his sinister arrows at you because the Truth is: *The Enemy loves to get us to live anywhere but <u>right now</u>.*

The Enemy loves to get us to live anywhere but right now.

C.S. Lewis discusses this issue in his usual brilliant manner in *Screwtape Letters*. The demon, Screwtape, writes to his nephew, Wormwood, concerning ways in which to foul up the spiritual journey of humans.

"Our business is to get them (humans) away from the eternal and from the Present. With this in view, we sometimes tempt a human (say a widow or a scholar) to live in the Past. But this is of limited value, for they have some real knowledge of the Past and it has a determinate nature and, to that extent, resembles eternity. It is far better to make them live in the Future."[97]

Screwtape's infernal plan is to distract mankind from the present with any means possible. Trapping someone in the past, he claims, can work well. You can imprison someone in guilt or even imprison them in the "golden age" of their life. However, the past only works for as long as it is finite and filled with the actual evidence of God's hand at work in our lives.

> If the Enemy can get us to commit our thought lives to the hypothetical, imaginary future, then we will not recognize God's work in the here and now.

Far more destructive is the prison of the future—an entirely hypothetical, self-made existence. If the Enemy can get us to commit our thought lives to the hypothetical, imaginary future, then we will not recognize God's work in the here and now; we will not be living or thinking in the *present*!

The Deception of "Good Thoughts"

Notice how our thoughts, when predicting the future, are usually negative. Isn't that kind of odd? And some of us (people like me, anyhow) have tried to "outsmart" the Enemy by thinking "good thoughts." We counter the ominous

128

predictions with optimistic forecasts like "The plane will land safely, no problem."

In other words, instead of predicting that the future is going to be bad, I decide that I can solve my worry by predicting that the future is going to be *good*!

Wait! I thought we decided we can't predict the future, and now we think we are making ourselves (and others) feel better by again falling into the trap of—*predicting the future*! Only this time, we predict that the outcome will be what we want. (Some define this as "positive thinking.")

The Enemy *loves* this game. In fact, I believe the Enemy likes this "good" prediction deception even better than the "bad" predictions. You see, if you predict that your future will be bad (*not* what you want) and that bad thing happens, you say, "See, I told you so." But if you predict a good outcome (what you want) and you don't get it—then maybe you'll blame *God*. Your frustration and disappointment at the undesirable outcome can be turned into frustration and disappointment with God for not taking care of you. Enough thwarted "good" predictions might even turn you from God—and the Enemy would be elated.

Or maybe you'll blame your spouse or loved ones. The interconnectedness of our lives with those near and dear to us lends itself to complex blame games. This laying of blame on those we love for anything that does not work out as it should (or so we think) is rich soil for the Enemy's seeds of destruction. Maybe he can wreck a relationship. Maybe he can mangle your marriage. All these outcomes are great results from the Enemy's point of view.

Throwing Good Predictions after Bad

We do this to other people and the Enemy just chuckles.

My daughter says, "I'm going to flunk my test*!" (predicting the future with a bad result)*

We do this to other people and the Enemy just chuckles.

Then I say, "No, you won't; you'll do fine." *(predicting the future with a good result)*

The added "payoff" of practicing predictions with our children is the generational outcome—we get way more than we bargained for when we pass on this dubious "skill." We leave a legacy of false prophecy. Here's another example...

My friend says, "I think I'm going to lose my job!" *(predicting the future with a bad result)*

Then I say, "You're a hard worker; you've got nothing to worry about." *(predicting the future with a good result, with a little advice jab at the end)*

So where does this lead? What is the larger trajectory of this prediction addiction? One little prediction can grow and land us in the middle of—a pile of predictions.

Prediction Pile-Up

If this weren't reality, it would be humorous. But the following scenario, though perhaps a bit overdramatized, is the way many of us spend a tragically large amount of time.

So let's say I decide to predict that I'm going to lose my job and that thought causes me to worry. Here's how it might play out with a six-car prediction pile up!

My original thought: *I think I'm going to get fired!* (Prediction 1)

The Enemy smiles, then slips in a teeny, tiny unassuming question. It's really just a whisper—"Then what?"

Then I won't be able to pay my bills. (Prediction 2)

The Enemy again asks, "Then what?" this time a little louder.

Then my credit report will suffer. (Prediction 3)

"Then what?" the Enemy asks, with a Jack Nicholson grin.

Then I may never be able to buy a house or a car again. (Prediction 4)

"Then what?" The Enemy is grinning widely now.

Then I may never find a job, which means I won't have money to send my kids to college! (Prediction 5)

Now the Enemy is belly laughing. "Then what?" he screams!

Then my kids will never get a job and my wife will probably be so upset that she'll leave me. (Prediction 6)

The Enemy can barely breathe because he's laughing so hard.

Now I'm barely breathing either, but for a very different reason, and I feel a panic attack starting to raise its ugly head!

Now the Enemy is belly laughing. "Then what?" he screams!

It's a six-car prediction pile-up!

A Life-Transforming 30-Second Assignment

Here's your 30-second assignment: Write out a thought that you are worried about. I want you to choose one that causes you any sort of worry at all, anything. There's one rule: The thought you write down *cannot* predict the future in any way, shape, or form. Go ahead, write down what you are worried about, but do not predict the future.

How did you do? Pretty tough, huh? That's because it's essentially impossible to worry without doing what we know we can't do—predict the future.

PRISON BREAK!
Present Truths

So what is Truth? Let's start with James.

Truth 1: Here is what I know—*I know that I have no idea what's going to happen tomorrow and I know I cannot predict the future.*

That's right. I don't know if tomorrow (or four hours from now or five minutes from now) something good or bad is going to happen. I have no idea! I don't know if I'm going to get my way or not get my way. But here is what I do know: *"I don't know the first thing about tomorrow."*[98]

Truth 2: *My life and thoughts are absorbed exclusively with God in this present moment and what he's doing right now.*

God doesn't live with me in my past or future. (Yes, He will be there in the future, but He's not living with me in the future; He's living with me now.) God is the only one who is the Alpha and Omega, but I can only live with Him here and now.

> God is the only one who is the Alpha and Omega, but I can only live with Him here and now.

Jesus said, "Give your attention (this means think about it!) to what God is doing right now, and don't get worked up about what may or may not happen tomorrow. God will help you deal with whatever hard things come up when the time comes."[99]

Truth 3: *I don't care what happens tomorrow!*

I know the third one's a little tougher, but let's give it a try. Let's try to let go of the future. Let's release our anxiety. If what happens is good, so be it. If it's bad, then I'll learn from it. If it's death, then I'll join My Father. So, Satan—go (back) to hell and stay away!

Sure, this is a hard view of your future to fully embrace. But truthfully, it's the only biblical perspective. Proof? Let's hear from Jesus Himself.

"If God gives such attention to the appearance of wildflowers—most of which are never even seen—then don't you think he'll attend to you, take pride in you, do his best for you?"[100]

Jesus went on to say, *"What I'm trying to do is get you to relax, to not be so preoccupied with getting (in the future), so you can respond to God's giving (right NOW!)"*[101]

> These are the Truths that should be taped to our mirrors, stuck on our computers, loaded on our Blackberries...

These are the Truths that should be taped to our mirrors, stuck on our computers, loaded on our Blackberries, read over and over. These are the Truths that can send Satan's worry lies packing—that can free us from the prison of anxiety. If we renew our minds...our lives will be transformed. It's a promise from God![102]

A STORY OF LIBERATION
Tim Lost His Job
Tim's Story

Tim lost his job. His response was typical of what many of us would probably feel—discouragement, shame, and perhaps more than anything else, anxiety. What was he going to do? Would he ever get another good job? What other letdown was waiting for him around the bend? Was this going to be the inevitable pattern of his life?

I had met with Tim the week before; this was our second

session. The arc of Tim's reaction to his situation is especially informative to the discussion of the tyranny of living in the future.

"Tim, last week we discussed a difficult situation you were going through—losing your job. We identified that as your challenge and highlighted the unhealthy emotions you were feeling. Next you spent some time figuring out what thoughts you were thinking that made you feel so bad. Then you took those thoughts captive."[103]

"Yeah, I wrote them all down.

"Do you still have the worksheet you started last week?"

(*Find an example of the original Lives Transforming Worksheet on the next page.*)

"Yep, it's right here. I picked one of my thoughts to work on and I wrote down how much I believed that thought. I believed it 100%."

"Great," I replied.

"But what do I do now?"

"We'll get to that. But before we do, I want to make sure something is clear."

"What's that?"

I'll never find a job and without a job I'm a worthless loser.

"The thought you chose—'I'll never find a job and without a job I'm a worthless loser'—where is that thought coming from?"

"Oh yeah, we talked a little about that last week. The thought has to be coming from the Enemy, doesn't it?"

"Why do you think it comes from the Enemy?" I asked.

"Because that thought is creating all kinds of emotional strife in my life, and *strife* doesn't come from God! It's not a fruit of the Spirit."

LIVES transforming
Your Life. Complete. Now.

LIVES TRANSFORMING WORKSHEET (The 4 Steps)
T-E-A MOVEMENT (Thoughts - Emotions - Actions)
THE CHALLENGE (THE GIFT - JAMES 1:2-4) (write it below)

IDENTIFY THE UNHEALTHY EMOTION (Highlight or Circle ALL that apply) - Galatians 5:19-23

ANGER	Hateful, Critical, Annoyed, Irritated, Skeptical, Other _____
	Angry, Selfish, Frustrated, Jealous, Envious, Other _____
	Hostile, Resentful, Hurt, Sarcastic, Distant, Other
FEAR	**Anxious**, Overwhelmed, Insecure, **Embarrassed**, Other _____
	Submissive, Inadequate, Helpless, Insignificant, Other _____
	Rejected, Discouraged, Confused, Bewildered, Other
SHAME	Guilty, Remorseful, Ashamed, Stupid, Inferior, Other _____
	Depressed, Worthless, Lonely, Isolated, Other _____
	Hopeless, Discouraged, Bored, Apathetic, Tired, Other

IDENTIFY THOUGHTS THAT CREATE THE UNHEALTHY EMOTION(S): 2 Corinthians 10:5, John 8:44

1	
2	
3	

CHOOSE ONE THOUGHT FROM ABOVE AND WRITE IT BELOW (2 Cor. 10:5) - This is your ORIGINAL THOUGHT!

_____

UNTWIST YOUR THOUGHTS

ENEMY LIES!	(A) Check all that apply to your original thought.	(B) Change the ORIGINAL THOUGHT: Take Out the Lie. Write a new thought (Truth) in the box	Belief %
Predicting the Future Deception	James 4:13, The Message		
Example of the Deception: "My son is late... he must be hurt."			
Playing Down Deception	Luke 22:24-26, The Message		
Example of the Deception: I just got an A and think "I'm still not as good as my friend."			
Playing Up Deception	I Corinthians 12:19-24, The Message		
Example of the Deception: I just got and A and think "I'm the best ever."			
Emotional Deception	Philippians 1:9, Colossians 3:5, The Message		
Example of the Deception: I "I feel bad so life is bad."			
Blaming Myself Deception	John 9:1-5, The Message		
Example of the Deception: "My husband got drunk... I made him mad and caused him to do it."			
Blaming Others Deception	John 9:1-5, The Message		
Example of the Deception: "I screamed at my son... his actions made me do it."			
Name Calling Deception	I Corinthians 12:12-18, The Message		
Example of the Deception: "My wife left me... I am a loser."			

The worksheets in this chapter can be downloaded at www.livestransforming.com

"Exactly!" I replied. "Galatians 5:19-23 is very clear that strife *does not* come from God. You can always tell you are thinking a thought that is Enemy-driven by checking whether that thought is creating unhealthy emotions. If so, you know the thought is coming at you like a flaming arrow from the Enemy,[104] intended to set our *Minds on Fire*! That's how we know the thought is a lie."

"I know, but the thought *seems so true!*"

"I agree. These thoughts can seem very true; they can be very deceiving."

"So how do I untwist the thought?"

"First, we need to identify the deception the Enemy is throwing at us."

"How do I do that?"

Demon Mentoring

"I was introduced to the Enemy's tactics years ago when I read the classic *Screwtape Letters* by C.S. Lewis. It's a book about an uncle mentoring a nephew. However, both the uncle and the nephew are demons. So the demon uncle is teaching his nephew how to 'properly' deceive humans with demon con-games!"

> "If I could predict the future, I wouldn't have to be concerned about a job because I'd just buy a winning lottery ticket by picking the right numbers."

"Is *Screwtape Letters* a Christian book?"

"Absolutely. C.S. Lewis was an incredible Christian author and a leading figure at Oxford University before he passed away in 1963. Lewis is probably best known for writing *The Chronicles of Narnia*."

"Yeah, I took my kids to see the movie last year, I think. But what kind of deception does Lewis discuss?"

"There are many ways the Enemy attempts to deceive us, but let's just pick one for now."

"Sounds good."

"Tim, can you predict the future?"

"What do you mean?"

"It's not a trick question. Really. Can you predict the future?"

"No. If I could predict the future, I wouldn't have to be concerned about a job because I'd just buy a winning lottery ticket by picking the right numbers." Tim laughed.

"Then why do you work so hard at it?"

"At what?"

"At predicting the future."

"I didn't think I was trying to predict the future," Tim replied, confused.

"Let me read an excerpt from *The Screwtape Letters*. The uncle, giving advice to his nephew, explains...

"The humans live in time, but our Enemy (God) destines them to eternity. He therefore, I believe, wants them to attend chiefly to two things, to eternity itself and to that point of time which they call the Present. For the Present is the point at which time touches eternity.... He would therefore have them continually concerned either with eternity (which means being concerned with Him) or with the Present.

*Our business is to get them away from the eternal and from the Present. With this in view, we sometimes tempt a human (say a widow or a scholar) to live in the Past. But this is of limited value, for they have some real knowledge of the Past and it has a determinate nature and, to that extent, resembles eternity. **It is far better to make them live in the Future.** Biological necessity makes all their passions point in that direction already, **so that thought about the future inflames hope and fear.** Also, it is unknown to them, so that **in making them think about it (the Future) we make them think of***

"In a word, the Future is, of all things, the thing least like eternity."

unrealities. In a word, the Future is, of all things, the thing least like eternity."[105]

"So the Enemy's goal is to <u>try and make me think</u> about the future and even predict the future!"

"That's exactly right. This is just one of the deceptive ways the Enemy works. Our job is to identify the deception and—"

"And then think about it differently! I'm not real interested in being deceived, but how do I even get started doing this?"

Destroying Deception

"Let's go back to the worksheet. So far, you've just put down your one thought. Now put a check beside any of the deceptions that seem to apply to the original thought you had that was making you feel so bad."

"Okay, let's see. Well, right off the bat, by saying 'I will never get a job,' I'm thinking exactly what Uncle Demon wants me to think. I'm thinking a thought that is predicting I will never get a job anytime in the future. But actually I don't know what's going to happen in the future! It seems odd that it's so easy to think these things that make no real sense!"

"I agree. Now put a checkmark by that one. And then go on and check any of the other deceptions that apply to the original thought you wrote."

"All right, let me try."

"I can see that most of these apply. So what's next?" Tim asked.

"Now you simply change the original thought into a new thought by taking the deception out of it. Try doing that with the 'Predicting the Future' deception."

"Okay…how about 'I don't know that I will NEVER get a job in the future. I can't predict the future.'?"

"Perfect. Write that in the box to the right of the checkmark. And don't forget to record your percentage of belief in the new thought you wrote."

"Oh, that's easy. I believe the new thought 100%."

"Okay, just write 100% in the box to the RIGHT of the new thought."

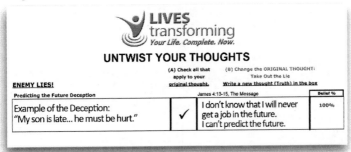

"Okay, now what?"

"Let's take a step back just for a second. Ask yourself if you still believe the original thought as much as you did when you started."

"No, actually I still believe it, but not as much. I believe it about 50% now."

"Okay, write that down."

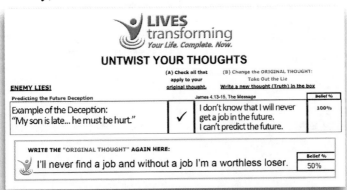

"Tim, as your belief in the thought that is making you feel anxious, rejected, embarrassed, and discouraged goes down, what do you think will happen with these feelings?"

"They will start to go away," Tim replied. "In fact, I'm getting a little relief from the anxiety right now. So what's next?"

"Now you can try changing your original thought for all the deceptions you checked."

"Okay, here's what my worksheet looks like so far…"

LIVES transforming
Your Life. Complete. Now.

UNTWIST YOUR THOUGHTS

ENEMY LIES!	(A) Check all that apply to your original thought.	(B) Change the ORIGINAL THOUGHT: Take Out the Lie. Write a new thought (Truth) in the box	Belief %
Predicting the Future Deception		James 4:13, The Message	
Example of the Deception: "My son is late... he must be hurt."	✓	I don't know that I will never get a job in the future. I can't predict the future.	100%
Playing Down Deception		Luke 22:24-26, The Message	
Example of the Deception: I just got an A and think "I'm still not as good as my friend."			
Playing Up Deception		I Corinthians 12:19-24, The Message	
Example of the Deception: I just got and A and think "I'm the best ever."	✓	Losing a job is bad but not the end of the world or the end of me.	100%
Emotional Deception		Philippians 1:9, Colossians 3:5, The Message	
Example of the Deception: "I feel bad so life is bad."			
Blaming Myself Deception		John 9:1-5, The Message	
Example of the Deception: "My husband got drunk... I made him mad and caused him to do it."	✓	I may have had something to do with being let go but there were other contributing factors.	90%
Blaming Others Deception		John 9:1-5, The Message	
Example of the Deception: "I screamed at my son... his actions made me do it."	✓	It's not all my boss's fault... I may have been partially responsable and the poor economy didn't help.	60%
Name Calling Deception		I Corinthians 12:12-18, The Message	
Example of the Deception: "My wife left me... I am a loser."	✓	If everyone who loses a job is a "Loser" then I guess I have a lot of good "Loser" company right now!	80%

107

140

Tim changed his original thought by taking out the deception and writing it next to the checkmarks. He was on his way to transforming his mind through the power of God's Word.

THE PARADOX OF THE FUTURE

As Lewis highlights so creatively and effectively, our access to eternity is in the present. It is not in the past—and it is most definitely *not* in the future. We are to give our attention "to what God is doing right now" and not be slaves to what *might* happen, whether positive or negative.[108]

The paradox of God's Truth is: The more we focus on the future, the more our present will be wasted, "missed." The more we miss the moment, the more likely the things we are anxious about will actually happen! Instead of this wasted worry, we can leave the future to the only omnipotent One who actually knows the future. When we do, we are promised by Jesus: "God will help you deal with whatever hard things come up when the time comes."[109]

God is more concerned with us than the rest of His creation; He *will* attend to us—there is no question of that.[110] So we can "relax" into God's present, appreciating what He's giving us

It's time to stop listening to "demon mentoring."

here and now rather than focusing on what we may or may not get in the future.[111] In this way, the hopes we have for the future *will* be met in God's divine form and timing, and all those worries and fears we might have will be outmatched by the assurance of God's hand in our present life.

It's time to stop listening to "demon mentoring." We do not need to "conform any longer to the pattern of the world" with its obsession with tomorrow and its anxiety-laced arrows.[112] Instead, let us be transformed by the renewing of our minds, no longer being captive to the future but living in the freedom of the present!

THE FOUR STEPS & TEA

To sum up, the key to breaking from the emotional prison of our past and future is summarized in four steps:

1. *Identify the unhealthy emotion.*
2. *Identify the unhealthy thought.*
3. *Identify the Truth.*
4. *Renew your mind*

When you renew your mind through His timeless and infallible Truth, you will experience transformation from God in both your emotions and your behavior:

T: When your thoughts change, then…

E: your emotions will change, then…

A: your actions will change.

It is for freedom that Christ set us free. God designed us for freedom. Embrace His perfect plan and experience the emotional and spiritual freedom through the renewal of your mind.

Additional Resources

Free "Four Step" worksheets are available from the downloads menu on the LivesTransforming.com website to guide you to freedom!

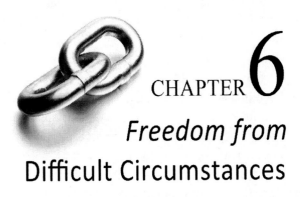

CHAPTER 6

Freedom from
Difficult Circumstances

> *"Consider it a gift when challenges come at you from all sides."*
> - James 1:2, The Message

THE PRISON OF CIRCUMSTANCES
Why Would God Do This to Me?

Courtney was devastated. A day before the sectional championships for diving—with memories of all those months of grueling practice leading up to it—a nasty collision with the diving board and an even nastier report from the doctor lit Courtney's mind on fire. As she lay there stunned in the emergency room, the doctor made it clear: She could not compete the next day. Months and months wasted. All the intensity and dedication, all the repetition and perfecting of her form. All for that one goal—and it was over in a couple of seconds. Clearly God was angry with her....

Matt came home and told his mother that he'd quit the team. No more middle school cross country for him. He was turning his back on a sport he still loved. The reason? He had developed a deep fear that had become overwhelming in the last few months. It was extreme, he knew, but he could not shake it. He believed he was going to die, to drop dead out there somewhere in the "country."

Though this might sound irrational from the outside looking in, anyone who knew Matt and his history knew his fear of untimely, unexpected death was quite rational. His father, in his thirties, had died suddenly—without so much as a hint of a problem—on a soccer field. These dire circumstances left Matt paralyzed in fear of life's trap doors.

Solomon's Quandary

In Ecclesiastes, Solomon declares something we all know but hate to admit: In this life, good people are often treated as though they were wicked, and wicked people are often treated as though they were good. This is so meaningless![113]

> If the world can't be perfect because of the sin that entered it at the Fall, can't it at least be fair?

Why does God allow (or perhaps even *want*?) things to be this way? If the world can't be *perfect* because of the sin that entered it at the Fall, can't it at least be *fair*?

People who don't deserve it get rewarded. People who work diligently for a goal—like a diving championship—never get their chance. Fathers die way before their time. Our circumstances far too often seem utterly unfair!

Ecclesiastes is, in many ways, a dark book. It's surprising that way. The common refrain "meaningless!" is pronounced over and over until it's hard to see past it. It's a stunningly stark motif for a book of the Bible. Are unfair circumstances proof that day-to-day life really is meaningless?

Most of us believe God has an eternal plan for us. But if we're honest, we probably spend more time doubting His temporal plan than resting in confidence in His management of our day-to-day affairs. If we're honest with ourselves, most of us probably think something like: *God's too busy to be concerned with me right here and right now.* Have you ever thought that? Or maybe the question is: *How often* have you thought that? More often than not? We know in our heads this is not the Truth, but do we really *know* it?

Blood, Sweat, and Tears

Jesus Himself underwent moments where He *seems* to have been overcome with frustration at the unfairness of life. Now before you start screaming blasphemy, let's look at three famous moments from His life: the death of Lazarus, the outburst in the temple, and the prayer in the garden.

"When Jesus saw her weeping and saw the other people wailing with her, a deep anger welled up within Him, and He was deeply troubled. 'Where have you put him?' He asked them. They told Him, 'Lord, come and see.' Then Jesus wept." [114]

Jesus wept? God in the flesh wept? Is this Jesus feeling the weight of tragic circumstances and being overwhelmed by the sorrows of the world? Suffering the anguish of worldly loss? The shortest verse in the Bible, "Then Jesus wept," could be one of the most far-reaching in its implications.

> The shortest verse in the Bible could be one of the most far-reaching in its implications.

Or try this one: "On reaching Jerusalem, Jesus entered the temple area and began driving out those who were buying and selling there. He overturned the tables of the money changers and the benches of those selling doves, and would not allow anyone to carry merchandise through the temple courts."[115]

Is this Jesus allowing circumstances to catch Him off guard and send Him into a (righteous) rage? Could this really be the Son of God lashing out in the frustration of the moment?

But of the three examples, perhaps this one is the most famous: "They went to a place called Gethsemane, and Jesus said to His disciples, 'Sit here while I pray.' He took Peter, James, and John along, and he began to be deeply distressed and troubled. 'My soul is overwhelmed with sorrow to the point of death,' He said to them, 'Stay here and keep watch.'"[116]

What follows is Jesus praying with such force and passion that He sweats blood. God of the Universe in the flesh fraught with sorrow. How could this be?

These three moments are remarkable, even startling. What are we to make of them?

Well, first, let me set the record straight. The life of Jesus is the only perfect life in human history. He is fully God and fully man, and from first to last fully righteous and holy. These three famous moments are *not* mistakes. Christ is not "caving in" to the human experience in any way that is imperfect or sinful. He "knew no sin." In fact, these moments are further proof of His supreme righteousness![117] In the end, each of these points of selfless compassion or righteous anger or pious suffering is an example of Christ the man worshipping, through personal sacrifice, God the Father. These are examples of *why* we worship Christ: because He *knows* the pain of humanity, He *knows* the weight of human compassion, frustration, and sacrifice.

But where do *we* fit in? How does watching Him handle this

pain, suffering, and frustration with the unfairness of life speak to us as believers?

The answer is simple, but infinitely deep. These three moments are confirmation that God's perfect plan involves blood, sweat, and tears. Jesus proved this to us once and for all.

The Circumstantial Lie

Like all psychological and spiritual prisons, the Prison of Circumstances is a prison founded on a lie. The first is the fairness lie.

Question: What makes you think life should be fair for everybody? Really. Where did you get that idea? What exactly do you mean by *fair*? Is there a quantifiable equation for fair? The

> Like all psychological and spiritual prisons, the Prison of Circumstances is a prison founded on a lie.

more you think about this, the more "fuzzy" the math gets.

One of the great lies of the human experience is that life should be fair. There is a kernel of truth here, but the breakdown is in the definition. If "fair" means that God in His perfect, divine judgment will set all things right for eternity, then we are correct to say that (eternal) life is "fair." However, that's usually *not* what we mean by fair. We really mean the circumstances of our life should align or balance with our own "good" or "right" actions. If this is what we mean by "fair," then we are in trouble.

A few more questions: How exactly do we weigh "good" circumstances as opposed to "bad" circumstances? Is there an equation for how many good circumstances should surround those who "do good"? And what is a "fair" degree of punishment for "bad action"? Fuzzy math indeed.

If God created a world that was completely fair and perfect, then the first thing He would have to do is eliminate the possibility of any of its inhabitants doing anything unfair and imperfect. A *fair* world has no room for pride, anger, selfishness, hatred, murder, or manipulation because all of these things are *unfair* toward others. And if all sin had a direct and *fair* worldly consequence, then there would be no place for God's gloriously *unfair* grace. If there was a real "equation for fairness," there would be no room for an "equation of grace."

> If all sin had a direct and fair worldly consequence, then there would be no place for God's gloriously unfair grace.

For God to take away the "unfairness" of life, the frustrating and painful and distressing aspects of life, He would have to take away our ability to *be* unfair. After all, aren't *we* ultimately the source of life's unfairness? He would have to take away our free will because, by definition, free will must be fallible. That's the "free" part. The ability to choose wrongly, to treat unfairly, to love or hate the wrong things. This is a necessary possibility of freedom.

PRISON BREAK!
The Hard Truth (and the Eternal Truth)

We know the Truth will set us free. So what is the Truth about the circumstances of our lives? The reality of our daily circumstances can be summed up in a cliché: "Life is tough."

Sure, we have moments of comfort and ease, but often our lot is hardship, pain, and turmoil. Christ tells us in simple, direct terms, "In this world you will have trouble."[118] It doesn't get any more straightforward than that. Life will bring "trouble." In other words, life will be "unfair."

But, praise God, in the "equation of grace," trouble or unfairness is not the full story. Christ finishes the thought with a word of encouragement: "But take heart! I have overcome the world!"[119]

Christ's triumph over the world is the reason we do not have to remain trapped in the Prison of Circumstances. We can look at the "troubles" of life, at its "unfair" moments, with confidence and an anticipation of God's eternal design.

Paul speaks many times about seeing the circumstances of life through an eternal perspective. "There's more to come: We continue to shout our praise even when we're hemmed in with troubles, because *we know how troubles can develop passionate patience in us, and how that patience in turn forges the tempered steel of virtue, keeping us alert for whatever God will do next.*"[120]

"Shouting praise" in the midst of troubles—a far cry from complaining about unfairness. By seeing the big picture, the eternal plan encompassing his daily circumstances, Paul says that he is able to find peace and contentment—even joy—in *all* degrees of good and bad circumstances:

"Not that I speak from want, *for I have learned to be content in whatever circumstances I am.* I know how to get along with humble means, and I also know how to live in prosperity; in any and every circumstance I have learned the secret of being filled and going hungry, both of having abundance and suffering need. I can do all things through Him who strengthens me."[121]

Paul makes it as clear as he can; he states that he is content "in whatever circumstances" and, again, "in any and every circumstance." The circumstances of life have no bearing on his contentment in Christ.

James elaborates upon this idea in his letter: "Dear brothers and sisters, *when troubles come your way, consider it an opportunity for great joy.* For you know that when your faith is

> When troubles come your way, consider it an opportunity for great joy.

tested, your endurance has a chance to grow. So let it grow, for when your endurance is fully developed, you will be perfect and complete, needing nothing."[122]

Notice the strength of James' statement: The "trouble" that Christ told us *will* come is an "opportunity for *great joy*"! This is truly counterintuitive, one of the great paradoxes of God's plan. But James doesn't leave us hanging. He explains *why* we should see the "unfairness" of life as a source of great joy: The testing of faith grows our endurance, which is key in God's perfecting and completion of us.

Paul and James have confidence in God's plan. They heard Jesus loud and clear. But more importantly, they were witnesses of His very real love. James firsthand, Paul on the road to Damascus. Paul's confidence in God's plan was a confidence in Christ, who promises to bring us rest and contentment amidst the blood, sweat, and tears.

"Are you tired? Worn out? Burned out on religion? Come to me. Get away with me and you'll recover your life. I'll show you how to take a real rest. Walk with me and work with me— watch how I do it. Learn the unforced rhythms of grace. I won't lay anything heavy or ill-fitting on you. Keep company with me and you'll learn to live freely and lightly."[123]

> Keep company with me and you'll learn to live freely and lightly.

The God who has experienced *in the flesh* the "troubles," the sorrows, the sufferings, the pain, the frustrations, the "unfairness" of life in this world is *the only* God in whom we can put our complete and utter trust.

His commiseration with us, His personal connectedness with and compassion for our own experience, is a miraculous demonstration of His profound love for us. In the end, Paul's ability to truly trust God's plans in the here and now stems from his certainty of His love for us.

"And I am convinced that nothing can ever separate us from God's love. Neither death nor life, neither angels nor demons, neither our fears for today nor our worries about tomorrow—not even the powers of hell can separate us from God's love. No power in the sky above or in the earth below—indeed, *nothing in all creation will ever be able to separate us from the love of God that is revealed in Christ Jesus our Lord.*"[124]

A New Definition of "Happiness"

The false definition of "happiness" is equally as debilitating as the false definition of "fair." Paul and James talk about "contentment" and "joy"; Christ promises "rest." Notice the translators of these passages chose *not* to use the word "happy" or "happiness." There is a reason for this. It's that concept we learned back in middle school—"connotations."

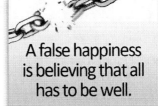

A false happiness is believing that all has to be well.

The modern definition of happiness has superficial connotations. It's a word that runs only skin deep, while "contentment" and "joy" are felt deep within. The idea that we should be "happy" in this life, that all has to be well, that we will get what we desire—is a false belief. As Christ made clear, this type of false "happiness" simply does not exist.

However, there is such a thing as an everlasting *joy* and *contentment* that starts today. Joy is *enduring* even in the midst of great trouble and unfairness.

To grasp this joy, we must empty ourselves of the need to have our way. We must believe that God is in control and that He knows what's best for us. We must trust His love, as did Paul and James and His Son. When we trust His loving plans, we will begin to be freed from frustration, envy, greed, jealousy, and bitterness—all the things that sap our joy. Instead, we will know the freedom of a God-filled contentment.

STORIES OF LIBERATION
God Manipulation
A Call from the Emergency Room

Friday evening I received a phone call from my wife. "We're here at the emergency room," she explained, "but everything is okay now."

My daughter Courtney grew up a gym rat. She started gymnastics at age five. With a state championship under her belt and a few trips across the country (and even one to China), she learned high-level competition at an early age. When an untimely foot injury shortened her childhood "career," the high school diving coach got wind of her gymnastics background and encouraged her to try diving.

Even as a freshman, Courtney was ranked in the top 20 in the state, and tomorrow was the first big varsity high school meet—the sectionals. If she did well, she would move on to the regional competition and then the state meet.

> We thought she was going to be okay, but soon the bleeding started and didn't want to stop.

"Yes, everything's okay now," my wife continued. "Courtney hit her head on the diving board doing a reverse dive. We thought she was going to be okay, but then the bleeding started and it didn't want to stop. So we're here at the hospital and they are putting six staples in her head. It looks like the sectionals will have to wait till next year."

The island in our kitchen seems to be a magnet for conversation. Courtney was getting her staples cleaned by her mom when she told me she had a question for me.

"Dad," she said, "I just don't understand."

"What don't you understand, Courtney?" I replied.

"Why did God do this to me?" she asked.

"Do what?"

"You know, I can't go to the sectionals. Why did God do this to me?" she repeated.

"What makes you think God did anything to you, Courtney?"

"I don't know; it just seems like God could have stopped this from happening. It doesn't seem fair."

Courtney continued, "I haven't been reading my Bible much lately or praying. But last Friday during study hall, I was worried about the diving meet so I got out my Bible and started reading. Then I prayed for quite a while—and then *this* happens!"

"Oh, so you think if you do your part, God should do His part," I replied.

"Well, I don't know, I guess so—"

Let's Make a Deal—With God!

"Interesting. So let me get this straight. You think that if you do the right stuff, then you can get God to do stuff for you?"

"It seems reasonable," Courtney said.

"So you think you've figured out how to manipulate God. You know, to get Him to do what you want Him to do?"

"Well, I wouldn't say that," Courtney replied, "but why'd God have to go and punish me? I feel ashamed and guilty."

"You think God punished you?" I inquired.

"Yes! But I'm not really sure what I did to make Him mad!"

"So let me summarize this. You think that if you do 'good,' you can manipulate God to give you what you want. And if you do 'bad,' you can manipulate God to punish you? In other words, you can negotiate a 'deal' with God? That's a lot of control you have there, young lady—especially over the God of the universe!" I smiled.

"I don't understand. You mean God didn't punish me?"

"Oh, believe me, Courtney, as Christians, we would all like to think that we could control God. Make Him bless *us* and  make Him punish—usually *others*. But we might be a little out of our league on this one...I'm not sure we have that much power!"

"Why then? Why did this happen? Why did I hit my head on the diving board *one day before sectionals*? Why do situations like this occur?"

"Because He loves you."

"*What*! That makes no sense. You'll have to show me *that* in the Bible!"

"We'll get to that." I grinned. "But first tell me, why *you* think this might have happened? Have you learned anything lately?"

"Honestly, I realized that there is probably more to life than diving sectionals. You know, Dad, I got myself so worked up for that meet that I couldn't even sleep the night before."

"Yep, that's just like your Father. He loves you so much that he allows you to go through difficult circumstances to grow you closer to Him and away from those things that pull at us from other directions, stealing our peace and contentment (and keeping us up all night!)."

"Okay, I understand. We've talked about this before, but

now it hits home. Challenges *are* gifts—"

"You're right—"

"Consider it a sheer gift, friends, when tests and challenges come at you from all sides. You know that under pressure, your faith-life is forced into the open and shows its true colors. So don't try to get out of anything prematurely. Let it do its work so you become mature and well-developed, not deficient in any way."[125]

"Here's another verse, this time from Paul": "There's more to come: *We continue to shout our praise even when we're hemmed in with troubles,* because we know how troubles can develop passionate patience in us, and how that patience in turn forges the tempered steel of virtue, keeping us alert for whatever God will do next. In alert expectancy such as this, we're never left feeling shortchanged. Quite the contrary—*we can't round up enough containers to hold everything God generously pours into our lives through the Holy Spirit!"*[126]

"But—"

"But what?"

"But what if I *intentionally* did something wrong. You know, like lied or stole something. Then God has to punish me, doesn't He?"

Punished for Adultery?

I opened up my Bible to the story about David. David was a guy who was an incredible king but decided one night to have an affair—to commit adultery.

Why didn't God stop David? Why did God let this happen?

Did God want David to commit adultery? Absolutely not!

Did God have the power to stop David from committing adultery? Yes, in a million different ways!

Did God stop David? No. God let David choose.

Did David's act cause some pain in his life? Absolutely!

Why didn't God stop David? Why did God let this happen? Because God loved David.

What? This Is Heresy!

Wait a second—think about it. God knew that David needed to learn a very important lesson. Although He didn't want it, God knew He had to allow David to experience the pain of his actions, which, in turn, gave David an opportunity to get his priorities straight—to turn toward God. God wanted a

This trouble you're in isn't punishment; it's training...

relationship with David. He wants a relationship with us. He knows exactly what we need. He loves us that much.

"God is educating you; that's why you must never drop out. He's treating you as dear children. *This trouble you're in isn't punishment; it's training,* the normal experience of children."[127]

This Truth is a knockout punch to one of the Enemy's favorite lies: "If I'm good, then God will bless me and give me what I want."

This lie comes in infinite forms. See if you recognize any of these:

✎ "If I live a good life, I'll have a wonderful spouse and live in a nice house."

Ask the apostle Paul about this one; he ended up single and in prison.

✎ "If I live a good life, I'll get rich."

Ask Mother Theresa about this one. Or any of the disciples for that matter!

✎ "If I live a good life, I'll get treated fairly."

Ask John the Baptist (who was beheaded) about this one.

> 🔗 "If I live a good life I'll quietly die of old age in my sleep after a long prosperous life."
>
> *Ask Jesus about this one!*

The Simple Truth

God doesn't necessarily give us what we want. But He *does* give us what we need. He *knows* us better than we know ourselves (and more importantly better than we know Him!). Thus, He knows our needs before we do and meets those needs "in mysterious ways," in ways sometimes unrecognized by us until way after the fact. The simple Truth is, He loves us—and *that* we can trust. Our

The simple Truth is, He loves us—and *that* we can trust.

job is to embrace the freedom of being freed from condemnation, being freed to be loved and guided.

Paul proclaims this freedom beautifully: "Therefore there is now no condemnation for those who are in Christ Jesus."[128]

The Worst-Case Scenario
Dropping Dead on the Cross-Country Course

For most of us death is the epitome of "bad" circumstances. It is the ultimate worst-case scenario of our daily lives. A few weeks ago, I was talking with a mom who was concerned about her son. She explained that her son, twelve-year-old Matt, wanted to quit the cross-country team. He was afraid he was going to get out in the middle of the "country," fall over, and die right in the middle of practice!

Now, what would you say to Matt?

No, be honest. Think for a few seconds and tell me what you would say if your son or daughter said, "I'm not running cross country because I'm afraid I'm going to die."

This is an interesting moment. All of us have experienced something similar, but have we really thought through what is happening in moments like these? So often, we give a clichéd response, perhaps a half-hearted truism or platitude. In this case, here are some parental responses one might expect:

"Oh, honey (nice sweet voice) you're not going to die."

Or, "Come on, you're NOT going to DIE!"

Or, "Stop worrying so much; you've got nothing to worry about."

Or, "You're not going to die; God will take care of you."

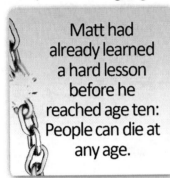

Matt had already learned a hard lesson before he reached age ten: People can die at any age.

Sometimes such responses will do the job for the moment, but they're just band-aids, and we may not see how far the cut goes—the deeper wound. In this case, Matt's mom knew too well just how serious the issue really was. She knew she couldn't get away with telling Matt, "Don't worry; you're not going to die on the cross-country course."

Why? Because Matt's dad, just a few years before, had died suddenly on a soccer field while still in his thirties.

Matt had learned a hard lesson before he reached age ten: People can die at any age.

Time to Take a Different Course

Tonight would be very different for Matt's mom. She decided to take a different course of action.

As Matt was about to go to bed that evening, his mom asked, "Why is it that you don't want to run cross country? Can you tell me again?"

"Mom, I've already told you a hundred times. I don't want

to run cross country because I'm afraid I'll be in the middle of nowhere and die."

"Die?"

"Yes, I would die and that would be horrible. I don't want to talk about it anymore."

"What would be wrong with dying?"

"What? It would be horrible!"

"Matt, if you died what would happen next? I mean with you, what would happen next?"

Slowly, thoughtfully, Matt replied, "I'd go to heaven."

"What would be horrible about that?"

"Uh—nothing, I guess—"

"So you're saying there really wouldn't be anything horrible about going to heaven?"

"No, heaven isn't horrible."

"So, what about dying—is it really horrible?"

"I don't know, Mom; I guess I've never really thought of it like that."

"Let's think about it for a minute. Let's say you are out in the middle of the cross-country course and you suddenly died—then what?"

"I'd go to heaven," Matt replied.

"And what's so horrible about that?"

"I guess nothing."

"Look Matt, if something ever happened to you, I would be extremely sad, but you are right. Heaven wouldn't be horrible. In fact, as you went to heaven, I'd be waving every day until I was able to be with you—and your father—again! Heaven yes, but horrible no. It would be okay; believe it or not, Matt, it's okay to die."

"Believe it or not, Matt, it's okay to die."

Matt's watery eyes dried up. As he thought about what was

true about death, he said, "Thanks, Mom."

Embracing Death—?

It would have been far too easy for Matt's mom to perpetuate the cliché: "Stop worrying, you're not going to die." But she didn't. It was odd at first to say out loud to her son that it was "okay to die." But after the conversation, the Truth was so clear. If only someone had conveyed that to her when she was Matt's age. What freedom! What relief that would have been—to believe something that true and feel that *free*.

Christ told us to "take heart!" for He has "overcome the world."[129] The greatest specter that haunts our lives is death, but He has overcome death as well. He overcame it by "embracing" it.

"By (Jesus) embracing death, taking it into Himself, He destroyed the Devil's hold on death and *freed* all who cower through life, scared to death of death."[130]

Freedom from the fear of death! *That* is true freedom from the most dire of all circumstances! God does not intend for us to remain slaves to this fear. Christ's intention was to "free those who through fear of death were subject to slavery all their lives"![131]

Lucky for Matt, the chains of slavery, the chains of being scared to death of death, were slowly unlocked with the help of a mom who was willing to avoid the "easy answers" and focus on the Truth!

THE PARADOX OF CIRCUMSTANCES
The Fairness of the Unfair

Why doesn't God want life to be fair? If life were fair, then all would be perfect. That perfect world exists in Heaven, outside of time as we know it, where the choices have already been made. On earth, it is our time to make choices, and because of that we have free will. With free will often come poor choices that make life difficult. If God took away all difficulty, He'd also be taking away our free will. It is in "unfair" times that we grow in character development—patience, kindness, perseverance. If life were "fair," we'd never have the opportunity to grow in these virtuous qualities and draw closer to God, and that is part of God's perfect plan for our life. The "unfairness" *is* the fairness in God's equation of grace!

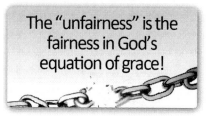

The "unfairness" is the fairness in God's equation of grace!

Redeeming Blood, Sweat, and Tears

Why do negative emotions like anger or anxiety exist? Without them there would be no weakness, which means there would be no sin, which means there would be no grief, which means there would be no love, which means we would have no free will. We would all be walking zombies with no emotion at all. We would not even recognize the fruit of the Spirit because without the negative we cannot recognize the positive.

What can we learn? It's normal to be angry sometimes; it's normal to be frustrated sometimes; it's normal to feel great sorrow sometimes. Christ experienced all of these things, but none of them for long. Why? He renewed His mind. Our part is to view our circumstances through an eternal vision.

True Happiness

The idea that we should be "happy" in this life is a slippery slope. False happiness is believing that all has to be well, that we get what we desire, that we experience the things we want when we want them. In fact, this kind of "happiness" does not exist.

We are designed to experience *joy* and *contentment* here and now. Joy endures even in the midst of great trouble and unfairness. The challenges, the "troubles," are opportunities for deeper joy in our faith in God! To grasp this joy, we must empty ourselves of the need to have our way. We must trust that God is in control and that He knows what's best for us, even when it doesn't make sense. We must trust His love. When we do, we will begin to be freed from all the unhealthy forms of frustration, anxiety, and pain. We will be able to experience the freedom of a God-filled contentment. Then we will know True Freedom!

THE FOUR STEPS & T-E-A

To sum up, the key to breaking from the emotional prison of circumstances is summarized in four steps:

1. *Identify the unhealthy emotion.*
2. *Identify the unhealthy thought.*
3. *Identify the Truth.*
4. *Renew your mind*

When you renew your mind through His timeless and infallible Truth, you will experience transformation from God in both your emotions and your behavior:

T: When your thoughts change, then…

E: your emotions will change, then…

A: your actions will change.

It is for freedom that Christ set us free. God designed us for freedom. Embrace His perfect plan and experience the emotional and spiritual freedom through the renewal of your mind.

Additional Resources

Free "Four Step" worksheets are available from the downloads menu on the LivesTransforming.com website to guide you to freedom!

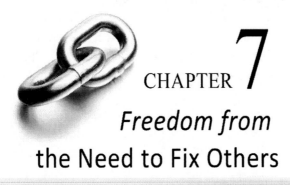

CHAPTER 7

Freedom from the Need to Fix Others

> *"Almost all of these attempts to connect and heal are not only naive and ineffective but quite self-centered and self-serving."*
> - M. Scott Peck

THE PRISON OF FIXING & CONTROLLING OTHERS

Consequences

Joann is one of the nicest people you'll ever meet. She's trying her best to be a good wife and mother...but there are problems. Big problems. She's beginning to suspect her husband is having an "emotional" affair. He calls her "a friend," but Joann's seen that movie and read that book a hundred times. But that's not the only issue. There's also the problem with her thirteen-year-old daughter. Lately Joann's found herself losing her usual "nice" demeanor around her daughter. She's even resorted to screaming. From every angle,

Joann feels like her family life is imploding.

Then there's Tom. Tom is at an impasse. Even though he's a pastor, it seems his daughter didn't get the purity memo. She's developed a habit of getting tangled up with the wrong kind of guy and it looks like the latest one is a druggie! Tom's thinking it's time for one of his famous (or infamous) "interventions." But he's having second thoughts. He doesn't want to push his daughter away; he cherishes their relationship. But can he simply stand by as she makes yet another disastrous decision?

> Lena's recently discovered some odd charges on their credit card statement . . . to a strip club!

Mike and Lena were an incredible couple. Gregarious, pleasant to "double date" with, full of life and energy. But Lena's recently discovered some odd charges on their credit card statement...to a strip club! A few phone-record checks later and Lena's uncovered what seems to be an affair. Why would her husband be lying to her? It seems something's driven a wedge through the heart of their marriage.

A Reasonable Enough Desire—Right?

We've all met a Control Person. You've got one at the office or at your church or at home. Or all three. Maybe you're that person. The person who thinks he can explain the issue clearly enough (or you might say "forcefully enough") so that people will finally understand what they need to change, what they need to fix about themselves.

The Control Person is obsessed with what others are doing and is doing everything he can to change them. But what about the Average Person, who just wants to help those around him? Maybe that's more of how you see yourself. Maybe you're not incessantly seeking to change others in obviously intrusive ways; maybe you are just concerned with *nudging* others toward the Truth.

Certainly that's a reasonable enough desire. There can't be anything wrong with "helping" others do better! Besides, it's biblical…right?

Fixated on Fixing

The fact is, most of us are *not* the full-fledged, card-carrying Control Person. We are—well, "average" in our desire to help those around us step toward God's Truth and a more God-oriented and fulfilled life. We want to see our husbands and wives, our daughters and sons, our friends and loved ones live well, love well, and grow in their relationships with God. That's a great desire, no doubt about it. But unfortunately, there can be a dark side to this desire. I call it a "fixation on fixing."

A desire to fix others results in frustration, distress, anger, distance, impatience, and of course, not being able to ultimately help (control) the other person.

The symptoms of this imprisoning fixation are many. And like all symptoms of false thoughts and "Enemy arrows," they run counter to the fruit of the Spirit. A desire to fix others results in frustration, distress, anger, distance, impatience, and of course, *not* being able to ultimately *help* (control) the other person.

The Adulteress and Her Accusers

Christ speaks a great deal about "fixing" others. One of the most famous moments is the incident of the adulteress and her accusers.

"Teacher," they said to Jesus, "this woman was caught in

the very act of adultery. The Law of Moses says to stone her. What do you say?"

They kept demanding an answer, so he stood up again and said, "All right, stone her. But let those who have never sinned throw the first stones!"

When the accusers heard this, they slipped away one by one, beginning with the oldest, until only Jesus was left in the middle of the crowd with the woman.

Then Jesus stood up again and said to her, "Where are your accusers? Didn't even one of them condemn you?"

"No, Lord," she said.

And Jesus said, "Neither do I. Go and sin no more."[132]

This teaching sent shockwaves through the religious leaders of Jesus' day. If ever people had the right to "fix" someone, it was at this moment. The woman had been caught in adultery (a theme of many of the stories in this chapter, by the way!) and the religious elite were following the Law of Moses in their "permanent fix." In other words, those who were there to stone the sinner were, by all conventional wisdom, *in the right*. They were correct according to the worldly ledger of crime and punishment. They were *fixing the situation*—and they believed they had God on their side.

> We pelt our friends and loved ones with righteous rocks and sanctified stones!

Sound familiar? How often do we step in to clean up the mess someone has made of their life? How often do we impose our opinions on their situation and attempt to take control? But the Truth is, our *solutions* for them amount to a metaphorical stoning. We pelt our friends and loved ones with righteous rocks and sanctified stones!

And what's the usual result of our newly "fixed" friends and family? Distance, anger, resentment—often even worse behavior than before. And what's the result for us in the aftermath of the inevitable failure of our fixing campaign? We feel ineffectual, unloved, useless.

It doesn't have to be this way. Just look at Christ's response to the impending stoning.

Christ turns the tables on the accusers (the "fixers") and exposes the root of their approach's failure. He points out their powerlessness to fix the situation outside of Him.

Throughout the Gospels, Christ persistently announces in diverse ways that the Age of Law and Judgment is over. The days of fixing through the Law are over. This new age is the Age of Grace and Deferment to Christ.

PRISON BREAK!
Advocates of Freedom

As Christ says, "I <u>did not</u> come to *judge* the world, but to save the world."[133]

We, as Christians ("little Christs") are to imitate Him. We are to be in the business of participating in salvation, not condemnation. Rather than *fixing* others, we are to be like Him, pointing others to *freedom*.

I love how Peterson paraphrases this famous passage from 1 Peter about the way we should handle our earthly relationships: "…summing up: Be agreeable, be sympathetic, be loving, be compassionate, be humble. That goes for all of you, no exceptions. No retaliation. No sharp-tongued sarcasm. Instead, bless—that's your job, to bless. You'll be a blessing and also get a blessing."[134]

Paul says something similar in Colossians: "…make the most of every opportunity. Be gracious in your speech. The goal is to bring out the best in others in a conversation, not put them down, not cut them out."[135]

Paul addresses this same issue in Romans: "If there are corrections to be made or manners to be learned, God can handle that without your help."[136]

"Forget about deciding what's right for each other. Here's what you need to be concerned about: that you don't get in the way of someone else, making life more difficult than it already is."[137]

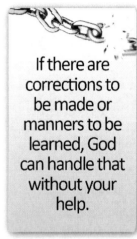

If there are corrections to be made or manners to be learned, God can handle that without your help.

The picture of our position in regard to judging and fixing others is clear: We shouldn't do it. Why? Because it doesn't work. The power and authority to judge and change someone are simply beyond our pay grade. We are not intended to be imperious inquisitors and hawkish prosecutors. We are to be humble and compassionate advocates of freedom in Christ.

Out of Control

We have absolutely no control over other people. Only they can choose their own thoughts, which then lead to their emotions and actions. Because we are not in the business of brainwashing and thought control (of others), we are left with a simple reality. We do not have the power or authority to control others. We are "out of control."

And what a great thing that is!

Think about it. You can't control others. What a relief! What a burden off your shoulders. The Truth is, if we have a desire to control others, it will eventually grow into an overwhelming weight on our backs. It will become the proverbial millstone around our neck if we let it.

Christ tells us to turn to Him and give over such burdens to the only One who can carry them.[138] Our job? To bless. To point others toward freedom. I'd trade the Control Burden for the Blessing and Freedom Burden any day.

Paul expands on this new grace-filled calling in Galatians: "Live creatively, friends. If someone falls into sin, forgivingly restore him, saving your critical comments for yourself. You might be needing forgiveness before the day's out. Stoop down and reach out to those who are oppressed. Share their burdens, and so complete Christ's law. If you think you are too good for that, you are badly deceived. Make a careful exploration of who you are and the work you have been given, and then sink yourself into that. Don't be impressed with yourself. Don't compare yourself with others. Each of you must take responsibility for doing the creative best you can with your own life."[139]

Does Freedom Really Work?

When we judge others, it closes the door to facilitate any growth because those being judged become defensive, resentful, or angry. When someone feels judged, manipulated, or not accepted, walls and barriers are erected. There is an extremely slim chance someone will make long-term personal or spiritual change in such an environment. Instead, these emotions block any chance of transparency, and community is broken. Look around; there are countless numbers of people who've been burned badly by those in church when they've messed up. Instead of being comforted, loved, nurtured, discipled, and restored, they were judged severely by those within the church. Certainly this is not the result of a biblical approach to relationships!

> Look around; there are countless numbers of people who've been burned badly by those in church.

By accepting and loving another where they are—with their mistakes, sins, flaws, and all—we build trust with that person;

169

we build a true relationship. God has designed us for true, trusting relationships. And it is only in a relationship of trust that friends and family will truly begin to open up their lives to each other. This greater transparency and freedom in relationships allows for greater facilitation of spiritual growth. Only in open and free relationships are we able to point others to the Truth of the freedom of Christ.

Does this mean that Christians just look the other way and pretend other Christians aren't living an immoral life? Of course not. But if we cannot approach someone in an environment of unconditional acceptance and love (meaning that we'll still love them just the same regardless of whether or not they change), then we haven't earned the right to confront them.

STORIES OF LIBERATION
Brainwashed by Religion
Yank the Radio Out of the Car

Joann met me at Taco Bell. I know—an odd place to meet—but my work took me to a different part of town that week. Joann is one of the nicest ladies I've ever met. Don't get me wrong, while "nice" isn't always a compliment, in Joann's case it is. She's very soft spoken, would rather say nothing than raise her voice, and she takes time to really think before answering. I could tell from our previous discussions she wanted to do the right thing. But she had grown up in a very strict organized religion and that made her current situation very difficult.

"How are things going, Joann?"

"I don't know. I'm really confused right now."

"Confused?"

"Yes. My husband says he doesn't really like how he feels when he's around me. He says that I've hurt him—but I'm the one that's hurt!"

"Whoa—hold on a second. Can you catch me up a little?"

"I think he's having an emotional affair."

"What makes you think that?"

"Well, he's basically told me. He doesn't call it an emotional affair; he just calls her 'a friend.'"

"When did you find out?"

"It was a couple of weeks ago. That's when he told me he was tired of feeling put down by me. After twelve years, he said he just couldn't take it anymore and he needed someone to talk with—'a friend.'"

> He doesn't call it an emotional affair. He just calls her "a friend."

"What does he mean by 'feeling put down'? Do you yell at him?" (Based on Joann's personality, I knew this was a ridiculous assertion. I couldn't imagine Joann ever raising her voice.)

"Oh no, I never yell at him. It's not like that," Joann replied politely. "He says it's the way I make him feel."

"Can you give me an example of what he might be talking about?"

"Yeah, I think so. I grew up in a home where we weren't even allowed to have a radio in our car because of the 'bad' music. Of course, I don't really like it when he drinks and—"

"Does your husband have a drinking problem?"

"Oh no, but he says I make him feel bad for drinking. And sometimes he'll watch TV shows or movies that I'm not comfortable with, and he's mentioned that too."

"What do you do when he does these things?"

"Nothing. I usually don't say anything."

"But he can feel something?"

"I guess so."

"Do you approve of him doing these things?"

"No, not really. I don't want him to do those things."

"So how do you respond?"

"I don't usually say anything. I'm pretty quiet."

"Which communicates what?"

"I don't know. In my family, when people did things we didn't agree with, we would simply remove ourselves from the situation. We didn't want to be around that type of stuff. I guess I don't know how to respond. What am I supposed to say when he does these things that I'm not comfortable with?"

It's About *You,* Not Him

"Why are you uncomfortable with him having a drink or watching certain movies?"

"Because I don't think it's good to drink and watch questionable movies," Joann said innocently.

"I'm sorry, that's not what I meant. I'm not asking why *you* are uncomfortable with alcohol and movies. I'm asking you why you are uncomfortable with *him* drinking alcohol and watching movies."

"Well, you know. Some of the movies out these days can be very risqué—and it hurts."

"I agree they can be very risqué. But I'm interested in why you are uncomfortable with your husband watching these movies, *not* why you don't like them."

"When he watches these movies, I know he's looking at women who are gorgeous and dressed provocatively, and it makes me feel—"

"Go ahead, how does it make you feel?"

"Like I'm not good enough."

"So the reason you have judged your husband's actions as wrong is because of the way it makes you feel?"

"Yeah, I guess so."

"And that makes you feel how?"

"Horrible!"

"Joann, you just learned something absolutely incredible."

"What do you mean?"

"You just learned that your judgment toward your husband is about you, not him!"

"I don't think I understand what you mean?"

"Joann, do you see that girl in the blue T-shirt sitting across from us?" Joann turned her head to look.

"You just learned that your judgment is about you, not him!"

"Yes."

"Imagine she came up to you and asked to have lunch with you tomorrow. You know—if she just wanted to talk. Would you do it?"

"Yes."

"What if you found out she had watched the risqué movie, *Animal House*, last night (yeah, I'm showing my age)? Would you meet with her or would it hurt you so much that you would have to decline talking with her and give her the silent treatment?"

"Yes...I would meet her." Joann laughed at the absurdity of the question.

"Why? Why wouldn't it hurt you so much that you would have to ignore her or stay away?"

"It wouldn't hurt me. Her decision to watch that movie wouldn't have anything to do with me."

"You're right. Her decision to watch that movie would have nothing to do with you not being good enough. What if your husband's decisions had no impact on how good you are?"

"I wouldn't be hurt."

"And you wouldn't have to use silence as a weapon."

"And then he wouldn't feel put down."

"I agree."

"Does this have anything to do with my kids?" Joann asked suddenly.

"Kids?"

Screaming at My Teenager

"What do you mean, kids?" I asked.

"You know, I really don't get mad very much and I very seldom even raise my voice. But the other day I just started screaming at my thirteen-year-old."

"Hold on! That's normal—you *have* to scream at a thirteen-year-old at least once a week." I laughed.

"Seriously, my daughter got in trouble at school and got a detention—it devastated me."

"Well, let's try again. If one of your daughter's friends would have received a detention, would it have devastated you?"

"No."

"Why not?"

"Because I wouldn't have been 'the bad mom.'"

"So your judgment toward your daughter resulted in you screaming because you felt like you were a bad mom?"

"Oh, my gosh. I did it again, didn't I? I thought my harsh response was because of my daughter getting a detention, because if she hadn't gotten the detention, I wouldn't have screamed. I thought *she made me* scream. But that's not right, is it?"

"No, it's not."

"My judgmental screaming was because of how I felt about *me,* not *her*! Unbelievable. The pain I feel comes from my judgments; that's what makes me so miserable!"

"Exactly. There's a reason why we are warned against judgment—it lands us in misery. *But most of us have been brainwashed to believe that our judgment toward another is because of that other person's actions.* Unfortunately, this is

174

powerful Enemy deception, based on his lies. The rage, frustration, control, manipulation, anxiety, depression, etc. that come from our judgment is never about the other person—it's about us.

"So how do I get out of this mess?"

"There's only one way out."

"What?"

"The way you feel about yourself can only come from One source—period. When you try to get from your husband or daughter the value and worth that only God

Most of us have been brainwashed to believe that our judgment toward another is because of that other person's actions.

has supplied to you as His child, you will feel significant pain from his or her actions. When those actions don't line up with what you think is right, your thinking may result in acts (sometimes violent acts) of judgment."

"Which pushes away the people I love the most."

"These lies always seek to destroy, not reconcile, relationships."

"So am I supposed to sit back and not have an opinion and not decide what's right from wrong?"

"Not at all. Use every ounce of wisdom and discernment God has given you to determine right from wrong."

"But how do I know if I'm discerning or judging?"

"Take your spiritual temperature."

"What?"

"Take your spiritual temperature. Ask yourself if you are experiencing the fruit of the Spirit—peace, joy, contentment. If you are, then you are discerning (healthy), not judging (unhealthy)."

"But what about other people? What if they aren't discerning?"

"You mean you want to discern for your husband?"

"I—guess—so." Joann grinned.

"You want to make others think what you think?" I smiled.

"Well, now that you put it that way—"

"I think God can handle them without our help."[140]

The Bible...?

"Aren't there verses in the Bible that talk about the fact that we should judge?" asked Joann.

Every one of you who passes judgment ... you condemn yourself.

"Honestly, Joann, be very careful reading any verses in scripture that lead you to believe you are to judge others! It's amazing how this deception can creep into our lives!" Read them in context with scripture.

And here are some verses that are helpful:

Do not *judge*.[141]

For God did not send the Son into the world to *judge* the world, but that the world might be saved through Him.[142]

I did not come to *judge* the world, but to save the world.[143]

Therefore you have no excuse, every one of you who passes judgment, for in that which you *judge* another, you condemn yourself.[144]

...who are you who *judge* your neighbor?[145]

Therefore let us not *judge* one another anymore.[146]

🔖 I mean not your own conscience, but the other man's; for why is my freedom *judged* by another's conscience?[147]

🔖 Therefore no one is to act as your *judge*.[148]

🔖 ...have you not made distinctions among yourselves, and become *judges* with evil motives?[149]

The Pastor's Daughter Is Dating a Druggie
The Chelsey Intervention

My cell phone was ringing as I was trying to scarf down a bit of dinner in my den. I was heading out to facilitate a small group, but I picked up anyway.

Tom's southern drawl gave away the fact that he was from South Carolina, even before I'd guessed the location of the unfamiliar area code.

"Derek, this is Tom. My friend Mike said I could call you."

"Sure, Mike mentioned you wanted to talk through some concerns you have about your daughter."

"Yes, I'm a pastor out here on the East Coast. At least, I've been a pastor for the last thirteen years, but sometimes (like tonight) I wonder if I'm qualified!"

"I'm sure a lot of pastors feel the same way, Tom."

"You're probably right, but I just don't know what to do."

"Bring me up to date."

"It started about three years ago. When Chelsey was about fifteen, she had a boyfriend who was not healthy for her at all. And now, three years later, it's happening again. She met this guy in Florida while we were on vacation and he's quite a bit older than she is. And yesterday I came across some disturbing correspondence on her Facebook page. I don't know—it seems like she always falls for these guys that '*need help*' or something."

"So how long have they been talking with each other?

"...it seems like she always falls for these guys that 'need help' or something."

"It's been a couple of months, but the language and provocative nature of their correspondence is totally out of control. My wife and I are very concerned and we don't know what to do. He's probably some sort of druggie!"

"So what did you do three years ago when you ran into this problem?"

"We had an intervention."

"A what?"

"An intervention," he replied.

I had always thought of an intervention as something they did at the Betty Ford clinic. And thinking of this poor fifteen-year-old having an intervention because her dad didn't like her boyfriend made me grin inside (primarily because there have been a few teenage boyfriends I haven't approved of either!). But I continued—

"So are you thinking about having another intervention with Chelsey?"

"*Yes*! That's what I'm thinking."

"What exactly is an intervention at your household? What does that mean?"

"I'll take her cell phone away and revoke her Internet privileges. She's on summer break from college and living with us, so I have control over both her phone and computer."

"So how do you think Chelsey will respond to your intervention?"

"Hmmm—"

"Derek, I don't know how she'll respond," Tom replied.

"What are her options?"

"She could get really mad and rebel."

"I agree. And what do you think that would look like?"

"She is nineteen, so I bet she could find a way to get her hands on a phone or computer when I'm not around."

"That's true. At her age, she's probably pretty creative."

"Yeah, doing an 'intervention' probably wouldn't stop her if she really wanted to talk with this guy. But I don't know if she'd get mad and rebel."

"Okay, what are you thinking?"

"In the past, when we've run into this kind of problem and I've told Chelsey what to do, she's actually followed my guidelines, and it's worked out! She calls me her prince."

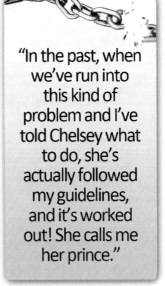

"In the past, when we've run into this kind of problem and I've told Chelsey what to do, she's actually followed my guidelines, and it's worked out! She calls me her prince."

"Like a prince that—"

"…rescues her from harm."

"Okay, what are the risks if Chelsey complies with your intervention?"

"I don't see any risks."

"Think hard…"

"Hmmm—I guess she wouldn't learn from her mistakes. Is that what you are getting at?"

"Not necessarily, but you are correct. She might not learn from a mistake if she doesn't make it, but can you think of any other risks? What is she going to do in a few more years when she's twenty-five or twenty-six and has a similar problem and she's not living with you?"

"I never really thought of that, but she'd probably call me."

"Expecting you to—"

"Rescue her." Tom grimaced.

"Yes, sometimes the only thing worse than rebellion is compliance. Is compliance what you want?"

> Sometimes the only thing worse than rebellion is compliance.

"No! I don't want to rescue her. I want her to learn how to make good choices on her own. But what should I do? Can't *you* just tell me what to do?"

"Tom, *if I told you what to do, I'd be doing the same thing to you that you are telling me you don't want to do with your daughter!"*

"Oh yeah, I guess so. Then *you* would be rescuing *me."* Tom laughed. "Boy, this can get messy. So what now?"

Out of Options

"Tom, what other options do you have?"

"I don't know. I guess I'm stuck. I think I'm out of options."

"I have a story from last year I'd like to share with you."

"Sure, go ahead."

"My daughter, Courtney, was about fifteen at the time and I believe it was a Thursday night. She asked if she could stay out late at a friend's house. I asked Courtney about her schoolwork. She let me know that she had a test the next day, which was Friday (but of course she was ready for it), and she had a diving meet on Saturday—"

"Well, I know what I would have said!" Tom broke in.

"I agree. The best answer seemed obvious to me too. However, I decided to let Courtney know that I wanted *her* to decide what *she* felt was the best answer to her question, based on the test she had the next day and the diving meet coming up."

"What did your daughter say to that?" Tom asked.

"Courtney replied, '*I hate it when you make me decide!*'"

Tom laughed. "That's hilarious. So I guess I do have another option, huh?"

"Actually, Tom, you have lots of options. And not every option is the best option for every circumstance! That's where the Holy Spirit comes in. Sure, weigh your options, get human counsel, but at the end of the day, listen for the Spirit within—and follow where you are being prompted to go."

"Still not going to give me the answer, huh?"

"No, you can take it from here."

"Thanks, Derek."

Where'd You Learn This Stuff?

A few days later I got another call from Tom. He seemed pretty excited.

"Derek, you're not going to believe what happened with my daughter!"

"What's that, Tom?"

"Well, my wife and I sat down with her and talked about what we found on the Internet. Then we let her know that *she* needed to make the decision as to how to handle the relationship with her boyfriend."

"And—"

"I couldn't believe it, Derek. This morning I found out that she broke the relationship off cold turkey."

"That's great, Tom, but..."

"But what?" Tom asked, hoping the other shoe wasn't about to drop.

"How would you be doing if your daughter *hadn't* made the right decision?"

"I think I'd be okay. I decided before talking with her that allowing her to experience the fruit or pain of her decisions was more important for her growth than trying to control or rescue her. So really, I think I would have been okay—not extremely happy, but okay."

"Great! Well, Tom, thanks for keeping in touch."

"Hey, Derek, before you go, I wanted to ask you one more question."

"Go for it."

"Where did you learn this stuff?"

"Jesus."

"Huh?"

"Yeah, do you remember when the scholar came up to Jesus and asked Him how to get eternal life?"

"Yes."

"Did Jesus know the right answer to the question?"

Tom laughed. "Obviously, if anyone knew the answer to that question it would be Jesus!"

> I decided before talking with her that allowing her to experience the fruit or pain of her decisions was more important for her growth than trying to control or rescue her.

"Do you remember how Jesus replied?"

"Yeah, now that you mention it. Jesus didn't answer; He asked the scholar what *he* thought it took to get eternal life."

"Why didn't Jesus answer his question? The scholar asked the most important question in the universe, yet Jesus didn't answer it. Why?"

"Because *Jesus knew that it was more important for the scholar to know the Truth (by discovering it for himself) than for Jesus to know the Truth and try to make the scholar believe it.*"

"Exactly. Tom, do you think you knew the best answer for your daughter?"

"Yes."

"But—?"

"But it was more important for her to know the right answer than for me to know it!"

"Exactly."

"Where was that verse again?"

Here you go, from the *The Message:* "Just then a religion scholar stood up with a question to test Jesus. 'Teacher, what do I need to do to get eternal life?'

Jesus answered, 'What's written in God's Law? **How do you interpret it?'**

The scholar said, 'That you love the Lord your God with all your passion and prayer and muscle and intelligence—and that you love your neighbor as well as you do yourself.'

'Good answer!' said Jesus. 'Do it and you'll live.'"[150]

I Caught My Husband with a Stripper
Love Unconditionally?

Mike and Lena were an incredible couple; my wife and I had known them for years. They were both outgoing and gregarious and lots of fun to be around. We had attended church, gone out for dinner, and had backyard cookouts together. They had two kids, they both had great jobs, and they lived in a beautiful house in a highly acclaimed school district. Life was good.

My phone rang at 8:30 A.M. as I was about to leave for work. On the other end of the line was Lena's frantic, but also angry and determined, voice.

"Mike is having an affair," Lena stated bluntly.

"Really? What's going on?"

"I don't know what made me do it, but I went online last week to check our credit card statement and I noticed some odd charges from very late at night—2:00 A.M. I didn't recognize the places so I called them, and you'll never guess—my husband has been hanging out at a strip club! He told me he had been working late so—"

I could tell Lena was holding back tears. "Lena, I'm so sorry to hear—"

> "So then I checked his phone records and there are all these charges to a phone number I've never seen or heard of. At 3:00 in the morning!"

"So then I checked his phone records and there are all these charges to a phone number I've never seen or heard of. At 3:00 in the morning! And I don't know what to do." Lena's anger was mixed with tears.

"Have you confronted Mike?"

"Have I confronted him? Of course I confronted him. As soon as he got home from work, I confronted him."

"And?"

"And he denied everything. I told the liar to get out."

"Where's he living now?"

"With a friend, I think. I already have an attorney lined up; she's a good friend from my women's Bible study group. She's telling me I need to cut Mike off financially and file for divorce as soon as possible. I guess I need to beat him to the punch so I can get a Christian judge who will take morality into account—so I won't get screwed. But I don't know what to do for sure. Derek, can you talk with him?"

"You really think he'll talk with me?"

"I don't know, maybe. He won't talk with anyone else. He's already cut off ties with his men's accountability group. I know they are praying for him, but Mike won't even return their calls. Satan must really have a hold of him."

"Lena, why do you think Mike lied to you?"

"Because he's a liar! He's lied before, you know."

"Okay, I'll give him a call," I promised.

The Voicemail

"I dialed Mike's number and, just as I thought, it went to voicemail.

"Mike, Derek here. I know you probably don't want to talk, and you've probably already been inundated with calls from your accountability group trying to track you down and fix you, but you know I'm around if you want to just talk—give me a call."

A few minutes later my cell phone rang. It was Mike.

"Derek, Mike here."

"Holy cow, Mike, I never thought I'd hear from you! I figured you'd be running for dear life!"

"Yeah, I know. I've had like twenty phone calls from guys at the church already. They are driving me nuts! Emailing me Bible verses, texting me their prayers. One guy tried to cast the "lust" demon out over my voicemail. It's crazy. I bet the whole church knows what's going on by now. Plus some of the guys in my accountability group work with me. My boss is a Christian— who doesn't take kindly to these sorts of 'acts of indiscretion.' They'll probably try and get me fired."

> "One guy tried to cast the 'lust' demon out over my voicemail. It's crazy. I bet the whole church knows what's going on by now."

"Man, the word got out fast."

"Well, of course it did. My wife goes to the women's Bible study and to 'help me,' she asked them all to pray for my lust problem.

Of course, all the women go back to their husbands and tell them what's going on. Then the next morning, I'm sure all the women have their phone on speed dial to get the 'prayer request' out."

"Well, I haven't received the email yet with you on the prayer chain," I chided.

"No kidding—'Pray for Mike because his wife caught him going to a strip club.' Can you imagine the Mary & Martha Circle getting that prayer request?"

I couldn't help but chuckle. I then added, "Seriously Mike—you want to talk?"

"Yeah, I need to." He sighed.

"Okay, come on over tonight after work. We'll head to the basement."

The Basement

"Mike, what happened?" I asked.

"About two weeks ago, Lena and I got into a huge fight. We were screaming and yelling at each other. I don't even remember what about. You know Lena has a strong personality and she's normally right, but she's always throwing something in my face. This time it was a knock-down drag-out until I stormed out of the house and slammed the door."

"What were you so upset about?"

"That's just it. It wasn't that big of a deal but I *hate* letting Lena down. I never seem to say the right things at the right time, and whatever I do doesn't seem to be good enough. It makes me feel worthless. I want a great marriage and all, and when she disapproves of me, it just kills me on the inside—it's really painful," Mike admitted.

"Okay, then what?"

"Then I went down the street to a local bar and ordered a beer. Someone had left a local newspaper on the bar. I opened it up, and right in front of me was an advertisement for a club."

"And you thought—"

"I thought, well, at least at the club someone will approve of me. I hadn't been to a strip club since I was in college, but I knew that if I pulled out a couple of hundreds, plenty of people would appreciate *me*...for once!"

"Mike, what if your happiness didn't depend on your wife approving of you?" I asked.

"I don't understand. You don't want me to care about my wife?"

"I knew that if I pulled out a couple of hundreds, plenty of people would appreciate me ... for once!"

The Question

"No, that's not what I'm saying. I'm asking, what if you didn't connect your worth as a person and your happiness in life to how much your wife appreciated you or approved of you? Then would you have to freak out when you got into an argument?"

"No, I guess not, but this is a little weird. I've always wanted to make my wife happy and—"

"I'm not talking about you making her happy. I'm talking about you needing her to meet certain conditions, like approving of you and appreciating you, to make you happy. And when she doesn't, then—"

"Then I get furious."

"And in this case—"

"I went to a strip club to get someone else's approval. I did it to make me feel good since my wife wouldn't approve of me or appreciate me!"

"Exactly. So again, what if you didn't get your value as a husband, man, dad, etc. from your wife's or anyone else's approval of you?"

"Then, you're right. I wouldn't have to freak out, and there'd be no need to head to the strip club. But how do I get there? What do I do next? How do I change?"

"You're just a thought away."

"I bet this is where God comes in, huh?"

The Lie and the Truth

"Mike, what's the lie you are believing?"

"I need my wife to approve of me and appreciate me or I'm a worthless man and husband."

"So when you inevitably have a disagreement, and she doesn't approve of you in that moment, you feel—?"

"Angry and resentful and underappreciated—not stuff that comes from God!"

"Exactly. Mike, what's the Truth?"

"I don't really know. How about 'I don't care if my wife approves of me.'?"

"Good try!" I smiled. "But this really isn't about your wife at all, Mike. Let's check out a few verses and try to get to the Truth. There's a verse in Galatians that may help."

"I identified myself completely with Him. Indeed, I have been crucified with Christ. My ego is no longer central. It is no longer important that I appear righteous before you (or my wife) or have your (or my wife's) good opinion, and I am no longer driven to impress God. (Because) Christ lives in me."[151]

> It is no longer important that I appear righteous before you or have your good opinion, and I am no longer driven to impress God. Because Christ lives in me.

"Okay, let me try," Mike said. "The Truth is that my value and worth as a person is connected completely with God. Because Christ lives inside me, He, not my wife, makes me valuable, so I don't need to be driven to impress her to get something out of her! I'm free to love her without needing her to make me feel 'worth more.' It takes the pressure off me to perform perfectly so she'll like me more, *and* I take the pressure off her to approve of me and always appreciate me—or else. I think I see this now. This really is awesome. I'm starting to see how this could really free me from lots of anger and help me see my marriage in a whole new light! But wait a second—Oh no—."

"What?"

"Derek, I haven't told you the rest of the story. After I left the strip club that night—something happened—"

The Next Morning

My phone rang at just about 8:30 A.M. again as I was on my way to work. It was Lena.

"My husband's lying!"

"I thought Mike told you about the strip club visit?"

"Derek, there's more. The credit card bill show charges to restaurants and stores *after* he left the strip club—and it's been more than just one night."

"Where is Mike now?"

"Staying with a friend. I'm not letting him back in the house."

"Okay, have you talked with Mike about these other charges?"

"No—well, sort of—I asked him if there was 'anyone else' and if there was a relationship and he said no. But I know different. He's lying. I didn't tell him I specifically knew about the other credit card charges. There's even a charge to Toys 'R' Us for God's sake! Then I tracked down his cell phone bill and the same number shows up over and over from 2:00 A.M. to 4:00 A.M.!"

"Lena, what's next?"

"I've had my attorney from the women's Bible study draw up the divorce papers and I've cut Mike off from all credit cards and bank accounts." Lena paused, "But if he would just stop lying! What else am I supposed to do? If all he's going to do is lie, we can't even begin to talk—it's over."

He's Lying

"Lena, why do you think he's lying?"

"You keep asking me that! I told you he's lied like this before. I think he has some psychological disorder, pathological or something—he needs help!"

"Do you think he's ever felt safe enough to tell you the truth?"

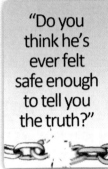

"Do you think he's ever felt safe enough to tell you the truth?"

"What are you talking about! Safe? I'm the one who doesn't feel safe! I'm the one that shouldn't trust *him*."

"Well, when he's messed up in the past and 'owns up' and tells you the truth, what—"

"Enough! If you're trying to tell me that *I'm* the problem here, *you* are crazy! I suppose next you're going to tell me that I'm just supposed to love him unconditionally while he's going out with a stripper! I think you're as screwed up as he is—this conversation is over!" CLICK.

Ruby Tuesday

The next evening Mike wanted to meet me for dinner at Ruby Tuesday.

"Derek, I don't know what to do," Mike started.

"What are your options?"

"I don't know." Mike gave a sad grin. "I'm out of my house, the bank accounts are frozen, and I got served the divorce papers today."

"What about coming clean?"

"You mean telling Lena the truth? Are you kidding? You don't know what it's like living with her. Every time I have *ever* owned up to anything, she's punished me for months and never lets me forget about it—ever."

"Mike, do you remember what we talked about last week?

Those scripture verses we discussed?"

"Yeah, about me not connecting my value and worth to whether my wife approves of me or not."

"Let me ask you something. If you disconnected your worth as a man from whether your wife approves of you, if you didn't *need* her approval because your Father has already given you all the approval you will ever need—could you tell her the truth?"

"Okay, that's a little weird. I've never thought about that. But yeah, if I didn't need her approval, I could come clean."

"So—"

"Geesh, Derek, I don't know."

The Apology

"Derek, I just called to tell you that I am sorry for hanging up on you the other day," Lena said.

"Lena, you don't have to be sorry. I understand how difficult this must be for you."

"I know but I just couldn't stand the thought of—. Anyway, I wanted to call and tell you that I've been thinking about what you asked me. I was doing my devotions this morning and I came across a couple of verses that reminded me of those questions. But I'm really confused."

"Help me understand your confusion."

"It's just that I want to love my husband for better or worse. I want to love him unconditionally, but I can't just let him get away with it. I think it was important to separate myself from my husband and protect the finances of our family—"

"I agree."

"You do? How is that unconditionally loving him?"

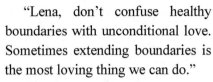

> "Sometimes healthy boundaries, like separating the kids or yourself from screaming matches and fights while things settle, or protecting family finances while you regroup, are the most loving thing to do."

"Lena, don't confuse healthy boundaries with unconditional love. Sometimes extending boundaries is the most loving thing we can do."

"What do you mean?"

"Sometimes healthy boundaries, like separating the kids or yourself from screaming matches and fights while things settle, or protecting family finances while you regroup, are the most loving thing to do."

"But how do I love him?"

"Take away the conditions."

"That's what hit me this morning. I realized I've been trying to change Mike for a long time. I wanted a better husband and family and marriage. And frankly, I've tried about everything to get that to happen."

"Everything, meaning—?"

"In retrospect, manipulation, passive aggressive behavior, control, anger, ignoring him—the list seemed to never end when I looked in the mirror this morning."

"It sounds like you've tried everything. Everything but—"

"Love. Love with no strings attached."

The Gymnasium

Well, it had been about a month since I'd talked with Mike or Lena and out of the blue Mike sent me a message asking me if I could meet him for lunch at Ruby Tuesday.

"Derek, you're never going to believe what happened."

"What do you mean?"

"Since the last time we talked, life has changed so much! But I'll start with what happened at the gymnasium after one of my son's basketball games. You remember when we talked about me coming clean?"

"Yeah."

"Well, I hadn't talked face to face with Lena in about two weeks. But finally, after the ball game, I asked if I could talk with her. Her parents took the kids home so we could be alone. And right there in the gymnasium, I just kept thinking, 'It's okay, it's okay—I don't need her approval; I've got all the approval I need already,' and I finally just blurted it all out!"

"Blurted what out?"

"Everything! And I mean everything. Down to the last detail. Oh man, was it ugly. What happened those evenings and about this gal I'd connected with—everything. I was literally shaking. I don't think I've *ever* come clean like that in my life. I didn't realize how much I've been tainting the truth over the years just so people would like me more."

"Then what happened?"

"She hugged me."

"What!"

"I know. Right after I told her everything, she looked at me and thanked me for being honest and hugged me. After she hugged me, she told me she loved me and then walked out of the gymnasium."

"Are you kidding?"

"I'm dead serious, man, and it about knocked me over! After she did that I can tell you—I realized in that moment I never, ever wanted any other woman in my life. I've never experienced love like that."

> "Over the last month, we've been talking honestly about these false beliefs we both are dealing with and what it means to love without conditions. We've been doing a lot of looking in the mirror."

Lena's unconditional love did the very thing she thought only control and manipulation could do—Mike changed.

"So just like that you got back together?"

"Are you crazy? That's just where it started. Over the last month, we've been talking honestly about these false beliefs we both are dealing with and what it means to love without conditions. We've been doing a lot of looking in the mirror."

"Are you back together?"

"Well, we aren't living together yet. I'm still living with a friend, but the divorce proceedings have stopped. I also have agreed to get tested; in fact, I'm doing that next week and Lena even said she'd come with me."

"Unbelievable."

"You can say that again."

Love Like That

But Paul can say it better than I can: "Watch what God does, and then you do it, like children who learn proper behavior from their parents. Mostly what God does is love you. Keep company with Him and learn a life of love. Observe how Christ loved us. His love was not cautious but extravagant (unconditional). *He didn't love in order to get something from us* but to give everything of Himself to us. *Love like that.*"[152]

He Found a Soul Mate—and It's Not His Wife
A Loss

What do I say to my best friend, a Christian man happily married for ten years, when he informs me he's found his soul mate—and it's not his wife?! He wants to meet for lunch at Ruby Tuesday. It's my favorite place to hang out, and I've met hundreds of people there for lunch over the years. As we sit down, he places his order and the waitress knows I want "the usual." My friend David looks up with a grin and tells me he's found his soul mate! What do I say?

Seriously, what are you going to say?

Let's assume I try to "fix" my friend and I respond like this:

- "David, what the heck are you thinking?"

- "Are you really just going to throw your family out the window?"

- "Don't be stupid!"

- "It's been ten years and you're just going to walk away?"

- "Come on, man, have you really thought through this?"

Or we can get religious and try these fixes:

- "David, you need to go to a Christian marriage counselor!"

- "Have you talked to Pastor Bob about this?"

- "Do you know what the Bible says about divorce?"

How's It Working for Me?

Let's assume I responded in any of these ways. How is David going to respond? Let's try some imaginary discussions (tongue in cheek).

Imaginary Discussion #1

"David, are you really just going to throw your family out the window?"

"You know, Derek, you're right, as I was rendezvousing with my soul mate last night, that thought never crossed my mind. But now that you bring it up, I think I'll call my soul mate and let her know it's over! I'm never talking with her again."

Is David really going to respond like this? No, that isn't going to happen.

 Imaginary Discussion #2

"David, don't be stupid!"

"Derek, you're right, I am being stupid. Give me the phone and I'll call my wife. I'll confess everything and go straight to marriage counseling!"

Let's face it; the chance of David responding like this is close to zero.

 Imaginary Discussion #3

"Do you know what the Bible says about divorce?"

"Holy cow, Derek! I can't believe it; I forgot all about any verses in the Bible that pertain to divorce. Do you have a Bible handy? Maybe we could have a little Bible study right now!"

Are you kidding me! *Never* have I had anyone respond like this. And believe me, if these responses actually came out of David's mouth, I would surely think he was trying to "buffalo" me to get me *off his back*!

 Imaginary Discussion #4

Okay, let's try again—this time with a dose of reality. What is David *really* going to say? Or at least what is he really thinking when I try to fix him, even if he decides not to say the words out loud?

"David, are you really just going to throw your family out the window?"

"You know, Derek, my marriage is already out the window. You're not going to believe this, but we've only had sex once in the last six months. *Once*! Now come on! What would you do if your wife was as frigid as Antarctica?

 Imaginary Discussion #5

"David, don't be stupid!"

"Stupid, what do you mean, stupid? Stupid is living with a control freak. Derek, you just don't understand. In fact, you're not going to believe what my wife did last week, she...."

 Imaginary Discussion #6

"Do you know what the Bible says about divorce?"

"Holy cow, Derek! I can't believe you're throwing the Bible in my face! Obviously I'd like to keep my family together but I just can't. I've tried and it's no use. Okay, maybe God will punish me for getting a divorce, but I'm not sure it could be any worse than the punishment I've been taking from my nagging wife for the last five years!"

Another Option from the Enemy

What's another option? How else can I respond to David? If trying to fix David doesn't work—then what?

Well, the Enemy will be glad to offer another option—a different road to go down. This road is one that *looks* like I'm supporting David, loving him and letting him know I'll be there for him through thick and thin. After all, friends do get divorced for various reasons. So I might say to David...

 Who am *I* to stand in the way? You know what you

want and I'll support you, whatever your decision.

Maybe there is such a thing as a soul mate. Maybe you're making a good decision.

This is messy, but I'm here for you anytime you need me.

Confusion

When I tell David he's heading in the wrong direction, he just gets defensive. He pushes back and shoves me away. But I'm the last person I want for him to be turning *away* from.

Two verses that talk about judgment come to mind. "Now accept the one who is weak in faith, but not for the purpose of passing judgment on his opinions."[153] And: "Therefore let us not judge one another anymore."[154]

I understand these verses now, because when David felt judged by my responses, he seemed to rebel! No wonder these verses are in the Bible!

But I can't just agree with what David is doing! I can't just tell him to go for it! No way can *that* be the right thing to do. What about these verses?

"...and the two will become one flesh. So that they are no longer two, but one. Therefore what God has joined together, let no man separate."[155]

"Anyone who divorces his wife and marries another woman (soul mate) commits adultery against her."[156]

I *must be missing something.* It seems so black and white. But it's as if both black and white are problematic. I either extend judgment and risk rebellion *or* I support him in getting on with it. Neither answer works! Is there another alternative? How can I possibly read *all* these verses and make sense of them *together*?

Scenario #1

So...what would it be like if I did *neither?* What if I just decided to try and understand David? Really understand him. Get into his world and try to see where he's coming from. What if I was curious enough about David's life to learn more?

Let's go back to Ruby Tuesday and try again. It might go something like this...

My friend David looks up from the table and says, "Derek, I have found my soul mate!"

"Really?" I respond "What's that?"

"What's what?" replies David, confused.

"A soul mate; I'm not sure what a soul mate is," I reply honestly.

"You know what a soul mate is!"

"No, really, I don't think I do."

"It's the person I want to spend the rest of my life with."

"Hmm...David, how is that different than a wife?"

"Well...I guess I don't know. (Long pause.) But here's what I do know...the sex was awesome!"

"So a soul mate is someone who knows how to have great sex? Well, maybe I need one of those too!" I say with a chuckle.

David looks uncomfortable. "Actually, Derek, I don't know. I sometimes just get so tired of the rat race of my family life. The grass is greener with someone else. But right now I think I'm just really confused." David lets out a heavy sigh.

> The Enemy loves to try and make us think the grass would be greener if we could just change our circumstances... our house, our job, our wife... then we'd be happy.

"David, I agree totally. The Enemy loves to try and make us think the grass would be greener if we could just change our circumstances…our house, our job, our wife…*then* we'd be happy.

"Yeah, it's probably a slippery slope. I may need some help through this," David admits.

"I'm not going anywhere," I reply

What Was That?

Was that judgment?

No, I don't think so.

Was it letting him get away with it?

No, I don't think so.

What was it then?

Before we try and figure out what THAT was, let's do another one!

Scenario #2

Here we go again. Once again, no fixing, no letting him get by with it. Just try and understand David.

My friend David looks up from the table and says, "Derek, I have found my soul mate!"

"Really?" I respond, "You've found someone special?"

"She's more than special; it's absolute magic!" replies David.

"So you feel good when you're around her?" I ask.

"Yes, it's incredible. I'm like a new man when I'm around her!"

"Do you think it will ever wear off?"

"What? Will what wear off?" David asks, a little confused.

"You know, that feeling that you have, the 'magic' that you felt last night?"

"I don't know, maybe," David replies, undoubtedly knowing that eventually it will go away.

"Then what?" I ask.

David sighs. "I don't know. This morning I was thinking

about how the feeling I have with my soul mate reminds me of the feelings I had when my wife and I were first dating."

"And that wore off?"

"Yes," David replies solemnly.

"I guess I don't feel in love with my wife anymore."

"David, do you think love is a feeling?"

"Hmm…I've never thought much about it. But if love is a feeling, then…. "

"You're right! If love is a feeling what happens when the feeling wears off? Will you have to move on from this soul mate to another one?"

David shakes his head. "Oh boy, the Enemy is pretty deceitful, huh?"

"You can say that again!"

"I think I might need some help getting through this," David says quietly.

"I'm not going anywhere," I reply.

What Is THAT? And Where Is It in the Bible?

Paul calls this servanthood.

Basically we just *served* David. When we serve others, it points them toward transformation.

We didn't judge David and we didn't let him get by with it. We didn't try to fix or convert him…we just *served* him (became a *servant* to him). Here's how Paul explains it.

"I have voluntarily become a servant to any and all in order to reach a wide range of people: religious, non-religious, meticulous moralists, loose-living immoralists, the defeated, the demoralized…whoever. I didn't take on their way of life. I kept my bearings in Christ…but *I entered their world and tried to experience things from their point of view.*"[157]

Let's look at this verse and apply it to our situation.

I have voluntarily become a *servant* to any and all in order to reach a wide range of people (like David): religious, non-religious, meticulous moralists, loose-living immoralists (David in this situation), the defeated, the demoralized...whoever. (Now Paul tells us how to serve.) I didn't take on his way of life (I didn't go find a soul mate or jump into his belief system). I kept my bearings in Christ...but I entered his world (David's world) and tried to experience things from his point of view.

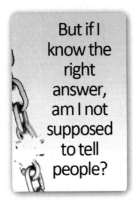

But if I know the right answer, am I not supposed to tell people?

But if I know the right answer, am I not supposed to tell people? Isn't that what Jesus did? No! Jesus' primary method of communication was to ask questions and tell stories (parables). Jesus was the Master at helping people discover Him (who He was) by serving them.

Remember the story we mentioned earlier? When a guy came up to Jesus and asked a question: "Teacher, what do I need to get eternal life?"

Do you think Jesus knew the answer to *that* question? I think so *too*! So what should Jesus say? What would *you* say if someone asked, "How do I get eternal life?" Was Jesus taught the "Roman Road" in Sunday school class (probably not, since Romans wasn't written yet)?

So what *does* Jesus say?

Jesus asks, "What's written in God's Law? How do you interpret it?"

Are you kidding me? Jesus *knows* the answer but He didn't give it to the guy, and it's a pretty important question. It could determine this guy's *eternal destiny*! What is Jesus doing?

He let the guy discover it for himself. Jesus knew the power of allowing someone to come to his own conclusion even when Jesus *knew the right answer*!

So how does the story end?

Does the guy figure it out on his own? Does the guy come to the correct conclusion? Does the guy try and skirt the issue? Does the guy try and trick Jesus with another question? Is the guy *so stupid* that Jesus finally gives up and tells him how to get to heaven after all?

> Jesus knew the power in allowing someone to come to his own conclusion even when Jesus knew the right answer!

Check out Luke 10:25-37 (*The Message*) and find out the ending!

THE PARADOX OF FIXING & CONTROLLING OTHERS

When we understand we are not responsible for fixing and controlling others in an attempt to change them, something amazing happens. We get out of their way. We create an open environment for others to self-discover Truth. And guess what? The change *we* were trying to make happen, one that could not happen in an environment of judgment, fixing, and controlling, actually happens in this safe environment of discovery.

Free and open relationships inspire free and open confession, advice, and a change of heart. Only in safe, open, and free relationships are we able to point others to the Truth of the freedom of Christ. By accepting and loving others where they are—no matter how clearly we see their flaws and no matter how strongly we believe we know how to "fix them," we help promote perhaps God's greatest gift: freedom. God has designed us to be free in Him and with others. We must embrace freedom!

THE FOUR STEPS & T-E-A

To sum up, the key to breaking from the emotional prison of needing to fix others is summarized in four steps:

1. *Identify the unhealthy emotion.*
2. *Identify the unhealthy thought.*
3. *Identify the Truth.*
4. *Renew your mind*

When you renew your mind through His timeless and infallible Truth, you will experience transformation from God in both your emotions and your behavior:

T: When your thoughts change, then…

E: your emotions will change, then…

A: your actions will change.

It is for freedom that Christ set us free. God designed us for freedom. Embrace His perfect plan and experience the emotional and spiritual freedom through the renewal of your mind.

Additional Resources

Free "Four Step" worksheets are available from the downloads menu on the LivesTransforming.com website to guide you to freedom!

FREEDOM VERSES

Scripture comes alive when read from the perspective of the "first person." I use first-person verses as daily affirmations to renew my mind. The following verses from each of the *Freedom* chapters have been converted into the first person for you to use in your own daily affirmations as you renew your mind.

FREEDOM IN CHRIST
Introduction

It is for freedom that Christ has set me free. I'm standing firm and do not let myself be burdened again by the yoke of slavery. (Galatians 5:1, NIV)

Let God transform me into a new person by changing the way I think. (Romans 12:2, NLT)

If I just use your words in Bible studies and don't work them into my life, I am like a dumb carpenter who built a house but skipped the foundation. When the swollen river came crashing in, it collapsed like a house of cards. It was a total loss. (Luke 6:49, Message)

It doesn't matter if others approve of me. My task is to be true, not popular. (Luke 6:26, Message).

For by grace I have been saved, through faith, and that not of myself; it is the gift of God, not of works, so that no one can boast. (Ephesians 2:8-9, NASB)

I no longer need to try to impress God. (Galatians 2:19-21, Message)

Since Jesus went through everything I'm going through and more, I'm learning to think like Him. I think of my sufferings as a weaning from that old sinful habit of always expecting to get my own way. Then I'll be able to live out my days free to pursue what God wants instead of being tyrannized by what I want. (1 Peter 4:1, Message)

I give my entire attention to what God is doing right now, and I don't get worked up about what may or may not happen tomorrow. (Matthew 6:34, Message)

My challenges are gifts. (James 1:2-3, Message)

If other people need to be corrected…God can handle that without my help. (Romans 14:2-4, Message)

It is God's will that I should be sanctified. (1 Thessalonians 4:3, NIV)

I take captive every thought to make it obedient. (2 Corinthians 10:5, NIV)

But the fruit of the Spirit is love, joy, peace, patience, kindness, goodness, faithfulness, gentleness, and self-control. Against such things there is no law. (Galatians 5:22-23, NIV)

I am from God and have overcome, because the one who is in me is greater than the one who is in the world. (1 John 4:4, NIV)

This is the one who came by water and blood—Jesus Christ.

He did not come by water only, but by water and blood. And it is the Spirit who testifies, because the Spirit is the Truth. (1 John 5:6, NIV)

FREEDOM FROM OTHER PEOPLE'S OPINIONS
Chapter 1

There's trouble ahead when I live only for the approval of others, saying what flatters them, doing what indulges them. Popularity contests are not truth contests.... My task is to be true, not popular. (Luke 6:26, Message)

I take up the shield of faith with which I can extinguish all the flaming arrows of the evil one. (Eph. 6:16, NIV)

Therefore, there is now no condemnation for me who is in Christ Jesus. (Romans 8:1, NASB)

God's Spirit touches my spirit and confirms who I really am. I know who He is, and I know who I am: Father and child. (Romans 8:16, Message)

Because of that Cross, I have been crucified in relation to the world, set free from the stifling atmosphere of pleasing others and fitting into the little patterns they dictate. (Galatians 6:14, Message)

I don't tolerate people who try and run my life, ordering me to bow and scrape, insisting that I join their obsession...they're a lot of hot air, that's all they are.... He is the head and I am part of the body. I can grow up healthy in God only as He nourishes me. (Colossians 2:18-19, Message)

For in Him all the fullness of Deity dwells in bodily form, and in Him I have been made complete. (Colossians 2:10, NASB)

It's God I am answerable to—all the way from life to death and everything in between—not others. That's why Jesus lived and died and then lived again: so that He could be my Master across the entire range of life and death, and free me from the petty tyrannies of others. (Romans 14:8-9, Message)

I keep open house; I am generous with my life. By opening up to others, I'll prompt people to open up with God, this generous Father in heaven. (Matthew 5:14, Message)

Open up my life. I live openly and expansively! (2 Corinthians 6:11, Message)

But if I am doing the very thing I do not want, I am no longer the one doing it. (Romans 7:20, NASB)

For I joyfully concur with the law of God in the inner man, but I see a different law in the members of my body, waging war against the law of my mind and making me a prisoner of the law of sin which is in my members. (Romans 7:21-22, NASB)

My dear children, I don't just talk about love; I practice real love. This is the only way I'll know I'm living truly, living in God's reality. It's also the way to shut down debilitating self-criticism, even when there is something to it. For God is greater than my worried heart and knows more about me than I do myself. And friends, once that's taken care of and I'm no longer accusing or condemning myself, I'm bold and free before God! (1 John 3:18-21, Message)

FREEDOM FROM FAILURE
Chapter 2

For through the law I died to the law so that I might live for God. I have been crucified with Christ and I no longer live, but Christ lives in me. The life I live in the body, I live by faith in the Son of God, who loved me and gave Himself for me. (Galatians 2:19-20, NIV)

I tried keeping rules and working my head off to please God, and it didn't work. So I quit being a "law man" so that I could be God's man. Christ's life showed me how, and enabled me to do it. I identified myself completely with Him. Indeed, I have been crucified with Christ. My ego is no longer central. It is no longer important that I appear righteous before you or have your good opinion, and I am no longer driven to impress God. (Galatians 2:19, Message)

If my perfection could have been attained through the Levitical priesthood (for on the basis of it the law was given to the people), why was there still need for another priest to come—one in the order of Melchizedek, not in the order of Aaron? (Hebrews 7:11, NIV)

When I live in right relationship with God, I do it by embracing what God arranges for me. Doing things for God is the opposite of entering into what God does for me. (Galatians 3:11, Message)

Its purpose was to make obvious to me that I am, in myself, out of right relationship with God, and therefore to show me the futility of devising some religious system for getting by on my own efforts when I can only get by waiting in faith for God to complete His promise. For if any kind of rule-keeping had power to create life in me, I would certainly have gotten it by this time. (Galatians 3:21-22, Message)

Christ lives in me. The life you see me living is not "mine," but it is lived by faith in the Son of God, who loved me and gave Himself for me. I am not going to go back on that. Is it not clear that to go back to that old rule-keeping, peer-pleasing religion would be an abandonment of everything personal and free in my relationship with God? I refuse to do that, to repudiate God's grace. If a living relationship with God could come by rule-keeping, then Christ died unnecessarily. (Galatians 2:19-21, Message)

For the creation was subjected to futility not willingly, but because of Him who subjected it, in hope that the creation itself also will be set free from its slavery to corruption into the freedom of the glory of the children of God. (Romans 8:20, NASB)

How did my new life begin? Was it by working my head off to please God? Or was it by responding to God's Message to me? Am I going to continue this craziness...? Answer this question: Does the God who lavishly provides me with His own presence, His Holy Spirit, working things in my life I could never do for myself, does He do these things because of my strenuous moral striving or because I trust Him to do them in me? (Galatians 3:2-6, Message)

God is love. When I take up permanent residence in a life of love, I live in God and God lives in me. This way, love has the run of the house, becomes at home and mature in me.... There is no room in love for fear. Well-formed love banishes fear. Since fear is crippling, a fearful life…is one not yet fully formed in love. I, though, am going to love—love and be loved. First I was loved, now I love. He loved me first. (1 John 4:17-19, Message)

FREEDOM FROM BEING USED—EVEN BY GOD
Chapter 3

Am I tired? Worn out? Burned out on religion? I go to Him. I get away with Him and recover life. He shows me how to take a real rest. I walk with Him and work with Him—watch how He does it. I learn the unforced rhythms of grace. He won't lay anything heavy or ill-fitting on me. I keep company with Him and learn to live freely and lightly. (Matthew 11:28-30, Message)

For You created my inmost being; You knitted me together in my mother's womb. I praise You because I am fearfully and wonderfully made; Your works are wonderful, I know that full well. (Psalm 139:13-14, NIV)

And the very hairs on my head are all numbered. So I'm not afraid; I am more valuable to Him than a whole flock of sparrows. (Luke 12:7, NLT)

Since I've compiled this long and sorry record as a sinner (both me and them) and proved that I am utterly incapable of living the glorious life God wills for me, God did it for me. Out of sheer generosity He put me in right standing with Himself. A pure gift. He got me out of the mess I'm in and restored me to where He always wanted me to be. And He did it by means of Jesus Christ. (Romans 3:20-22, Message)

By entering through faith into what God has always wanted to do for me—He set me right with Him, made me fit for Him—I have it all together with God because of our Master Jesus. And that's not all: I throw open my door to God and discover at the same moment that He has already thrown open His door to me. I find myself standing where I always hoped I might stand—out in the wide open spaces of God's grace and glory, standing tall and shouting my praise. (Romans 5:1, Message)

I live in Him. I make my home in Him just as He does in me. In the same way that a branch can't bear grapes by itself but only by being joined to the vine, I can't bear fruit unless I'm joined with Him. He's the Vine, I'm the branches. When I'm joined with Him and He with me, the relation intimate and organic, the harvest is sure to be abundant. Separated, I can't produce a thing. Anyone who separates from Him is deadwood, gathered up and thrown on the bonfire. But if I make myself at home with Him and my words are at home in Him, I can be sure that whatever I ask will be listened to and acted upon. This is how my Father shows who He is—I produce grapes, I mature as a disciple. (John 15:4-8, Message)

FREEDOM FROM WANTING WHAT WE DON'T HAVE
Chapter 4

...and in Him I have been made complete, and He is the head over all rule and authority. (Colossians 2:10, NASB)

For my part, I am going to boast about nothing but the Cross of our Master, Jesus Christ. Because of that Cross, I have been crucified in relation to the world, set free from the stifling atmosphere of pleasing others and fitting into the little patterns that they dictate. I can see the central issue in all this. It is not what I do—submit to circumcision, reject circumcision. It is what God is doing, and He is creating something totally new, a free life! All who walk by this standard are the true Israel of God—His chosen people. Peace and mercy on us! (Galatians 6:14-16, Message)

The Spirit of the Lord is on me, because He has anointed me to preach good news to the poor. He has sent me to proclaim freedom for the prisoners and recovery of sight for the blind, to release the oppressed. (Luke 4:1-8, NIV)

I love the Lord my God with all my heart and with all my soul and with all my mind and with all my strength. (Mark 12:30, NIV)

I can't serve two masters. Either I will hate the one and love the other, or I will be devoted to the one and despise the other. I cannot serve both God and money. (Matthew 6:24, NIV)

Since Jesus went through everything I'm going through and more, I'm learning to think like Him. I think of my sufferings as a weaning from that old sinful habit of always expecting to get my way. Then I'm able to live out my days free to pursue what God wants instead of being tyrannized by what I want. (1 Peter 4:1-2, Message)

As the deer pants for streams of water, so my soul pants for You, O God. (Psalm 42:1, NIV)

But now apart from the Law, the righteousness of God has been manifested, being witnessed by the Law and the Prophets, even the righteousness of God through faith in Jesus Christ for all who believe, including me; for there is no distinction.

(Romans 3:21-22, NASB)

But to me who does not work, but believes in Him who justifies the ungodly, my faith is credited as righteousness. (Romans 4:5, NASB)

On the contrary, who am I who answers back to God? The thing molded will not say to the molder, "Why did you make me like this," will it? Or does not the potter have a right over the clay, to make from the same lump one vessel for honorable use and another for common use? (Romans 9:20-21, NIV)

So where does that leave me when I criticize a brother? And where does that leave me when I condescend to a sister? I'd say it leaves me looking pretty silly—or worse. (Romans 14:10, Message)

I forget about deciding what's right for others. Here's what I need to be concerned about: that I don't get in the way of someone else, making life more difficult than it already is. (Romans 14:13, Message)

I cultivate my own relationship with God, but I don't impose it on others. (Romans 14:22, Message)

FREEDOM FROM THE PAST AND FUTURE
Chapter 5

I pay attention to what God is doing right now, and I don't get worked up about what may or may not happen tomorrow. God will help me deal with whatever hard things come up when the time comes. (Matthew 6:34, Message)

If God gives such attention to the appearance of wildflowers—most of which are never even seen—then don't I think He'll attend to me, take pride in me, do His best for me? (Matthew 6:30, Message)

What He's trying to do is get me to relax, to not be so preoccupied with getting, so I can respond to God's giving. (Matthew 6:31, Message)

I do not conform any longer to the pattern of this world, but I let God transform me by renewing of my mind. Then I will be able to test and approve what God's will is—His good, pleasing, and perfect will. (Romans 12:2, NIV)

I demolish arguments and every pretension that sets itself up against the knowledge of God, and I take captive every thought to make it obedient to Christ. (2 Corinthians 10:5, NIV)

In addition to all this, I take up the shield of faith, with which I can extinguish all the flaming arrows of the evil one. (Ephesians 6:16, NIV)

FREEDOM FROM DIFFICULT CIRCUMSTANCES
Chapter 6

In this life, good people are often treated as though they are wicked, and wicked people are often treated as though they are good. This is so meaningless! (Ecclesiastes 8:14, NLT)

When Jesus saw her weeping and saw the other people wailing with her, a deep anger welled up within Him, and He was deeply troubled. "Where have you put him?" He asked them. They told Him, "Lord, come and see." Then Jesus wept. (John 11:33-35, NLT)

They went to a place called Gethsemane, and Jesus said to His disciples, "Sit here while I pray." He took Peter, James, and John along, and He began to be deeply distressed and troubled. "My soul is overwhelmed with sorrow to the point of death," He said to them. "Stay here and keep watch." (Mark 14:32-34, NIV)

There is now no condemnation for me in Christ Jesus, because through Christ Jesus the law of the Spirit of life set me free from the law of sin and death. (Romans 8:1-2, NIV)

He has told me these things, so that in Him I may have peace. In this world I will have trouble. But I take heart! He has overcome the world. (John 16:33, NIV)

There's more to come: I continue to shout my praise even when I'm hemmed in with troubles, because I know how troubles can develop passionate patience in me, and how that patience in turn forges the tempered steel of virtue, keeping me alert for whatever God will do next. (Romans 5:3, Message)

Not that I speak from want, for I have learned to be content in whatever circumstances I am. I know how to get along with humble means, and I also know how to live in prosperity; in any and every circumstance I have learned the secret of being filled and going hungry, both of having abundance and suffering need. I can do all things through Him who strengthens me. (Philippians 4:11-13, NASB)

...when troubles come my way, I consider it an opportunity for great joy. For I know that when my faith is tested, my endurance has a chance to grow. So I let it grow, for when my endurance is fully developed, I will be perfect and complete, needing nothing. (James 1:2-4, NLT)

Am I tired? Worn out? Burned out on religion? I go to Him. I get away with Him and recover my life. He shows me how to take a real rest. I walk with Him and work with Him—watch how He does it. I learn the unforced rhythms of grace. He won't lay anything heavy or ill-fitting on me. I keep company with Him and learn to live freely and lightly. (Matthew 11:28-30, Message)

And I am convinced that nothing can ever separate me from God's love. Neither death nor life, neither angels nor demons, neither our fears for today nor our worries about tomorrow—not even the powers of hell can separate me from God's love. No power in the sky above or in the earth below—indeed, nothing in all creation will ever be able to separate me from the love of God that is revealed in Christ Jesus our Lord. (Romans 8:38-39, NLT)

God is educating me; that's why I must never drop out. He's treating me as a dear child. This trouble I'm in isn't punishment; it's training, the normal experience of children. (Hebrews 12:7-8, Message)

Therefore there is now no condemnation for those who are in Christ Jesus. (Romans 8:1, NASB)

By embracing death, taking it into Himself, He destroyed the Devil's hold on death and freed me from cowering through life, scared to death of death. (Hebrews 2:15, Message)

...summing up: I am agreeable, extend sympathy, am loving, compassionate, and humble. That goes for everyone, no exceptions. No retaliation. No sharp-tongued sarcasm. Instead, I bless—it's my job, to bless. I'll be a blessing and also get a blessing. (1 Peter 3:8-9, Message)

...I make the most of every opportunity. I am gracious with my speech. The goal is to bring out the best in others in a conversation, not put them down, not cut them out. (Colossians 4:5-6, Message)

If there are corrections to be made or manners to be learned, God can handle that without my help. (Romans 14:4, Message)

I go to Him when I'm weary and burdened, and He gives me rest. I take His yoke upon myself and learn from Him, for He is gentle and humble in heart, and I find rest for my soul. For His yoke is easy and His burden is light. (Matthew 11:28-30, NIV)

I live creatively. If someone falls into sin, I forgivingly restore him, saving my critical comments for myself. I might be needing forgiveness before the day's out. I stoop down and reach out to those who are oppressed. I share their burdens, and so complete Christ's law. If I think I'm too good for that, I am badly deceived. I make a careful exploration of who I am and the work I have been given, and then sink into that. I'm not impressed with myself. I don't compare myself with others. I must take responsibility for doing the creative best I can with my own life. (Galatians 6:1-5, Message)

I do not judge. (Matthew 7:1, NASB, and Luke 6:37, NASB)

For God did not send the Son into the world to judge the world, but that the world might be saved through Him. (John 3:17, NASB)

He did not come to judge the world, but to save the world. (John 12:47, NASB)

Therefore I have no excuse, if I pass judgment, for in that which I judge another, I condemn myself. (Romans 2:1, NASB)

But why, why do I judge my brother? (Romans 14:10, NASB)

Therefore I do not judge others any more. (Romans 14:13, NASB)

...who am I to judge my neighbor? (James 4:12, NASB)

I don't just put up with my limitations; I celebrate them, and then go on to celebrate every strength, and every triumph of the truth in myself. (2 Corinthians 13:8, Message)

I watch what God does, and then I do it, like a child who learns proper behavior from his or her parents. Mostly what God does is love me. I keep company with Him and learn a life of love. I observe how Christ loves me. His love is not cautious but extravagant. He didn't love in order to get something from me but to give everything of Himself to me. I love like that. (Ephesians 5:1, Message)

I have voluntarily become a servant to any and all in order to reach a wide range of people: religious, non-religious, meticulous moralists, loose-living immoralists, the defeated, the demoralized—whoever. I didn't take on their way of life. I kept my bearings in Christ—but I entered their world and tried to experience things from their point of view. (1 Corinthians 9:20-22, Message)

I identified myself completely with Him. Indeed, I have been crucified with Christ. My ego is no longer central. It is no longer important that I appear righteous before you or have your good opinion, and I am no longer driven to impress God. Christ lives in me. (Galatians 2:20-21, Message)

ABOUT THE AUTHOR

Derek Wilder

Workaholic is a word that has been used to describe me, but I would say "performance addict" was probably more accurate. As the son of a world-class shooter (whose legacy included twenty-four national championships and numerous medals in world class competition), I chose to listen to my dad's sports psychologist at the Colorado Springs Olympic Training Center, whose cassette tapes about "how we think" played on my headset while mowing the lawn at age nine. I was on the fast track from the beginning. But about the same time I was listening to my dad's tapes, I also was baptized. I went to church every Sunday morning with my family, but church seemed to be disconnected from the rest of my life. Even at the ripe old age of twelve, I wondered how my thoughts had anything to do with God.

During my freshman year of college, when I was thinking about what career path to take, I considered going into the ministry. I asked my father what he thought, and his advice was, "Work hard and make a lot of money. Then people will listen to you."

So I did. At twenty-one, I graduated from a Christian liberal arts college. Swimming in student loan debt, I landed a job with one of the world's premier consulting firms, Deloitte. At twenty-four, I started my own business, at twenty-five, I had my first six-figure income, and by thirty, I was a millionaire after my partner and I grew the business to one of the top five in the state. The more I succeeded, the harder I worked. "Winners make it happen...." I was determined to be in the winner's group, and losers who let life happen to them were my least favorite people.

I was not quite thirty when "it" happened. I'm not sure what "it" was, but I call it my own personal beautiful train wreck. My personal physician thought it had to do with my "emotions." I told him I didn't think I had any of those. Regardless, the "it" manifested itself in all kinds of physical issues: hives, swelling, numbness, waking up in the middle of the night in a pool of sweat...and why couldn't I stop crying behind my closed office doors? Of course, the first person I turned to was my wife...who quickly explained that she didn't like being around me anymore. So I turned back to my doctor who gave me some pills that "could be addictive" and told me I should "be careful" with them. He also suggested that counseling might be helpful.

My pastor agreed to meet with me. His first question was, "Where is God working in your life?" I told him I didn't know. After getting to know me, he identified me as having the spiritual gift of leadership. I had no idea what he was talking about, but I remember listening to a speech given by Bill Hybels introducing me to a God who gifts certain people with a Holy Spirit–endowed gift of leadership. You don't earn it, you don't work for it...it's simply a gift. I wept again...but for a different reason. All the worldly success would have been impossible without this gift. Hmm...my performance was never really mine...it was a gift? Maybe life wasn't all about me after all. Why did this realization comfort me?

A little confused and extremely determined, I hired a very talented executive coach. He was a Christian believer who continued pointing me toward God's Truth, which I absorbed like desert sand in a rainstorm. As an insatiable learner earnestly seeking physical, emotional, and spiritual health, I began to see connections between my life and God's Truth. When I realized my value and worth didn't come from my performance, my anxiety started to subside. I wanted to know more. I wanted to know HOW to get Truth inside my life (not realizing He was already there) and *how* to communicate Truth to others.

During the next decade, I learned a lot, mostly from men who had passed away (Oswald Chambers, Martin Luther, Watchman Nee, C.S. Lewis), and a few other contemporary ones (Robert McGee, David Burns, MD, and M. Scott Peck, MD). Not all are Christians, and I didn't agree with everything even the Christians believed, but each one took me deeper into the journey that brought me life.

These days, my telephone, office, and email inbox continually fill up with others asking the same questions that I had at that time in my life. Many of these people are desperate, and some are simply seeking. Some are pastors who have been rejected by their churches, lifelong believers who can no longer "keep the faith." Some are people who have never been to church but deeply desire Truth. Some are individuals who cannot find or even identify "love." Others are couples with decimated marriages, or children of those marriages, or people in financial bondage (poverty to wealth), or drug addicts, or abused women, or church elders, or homosexuals, or congressmen, or professional athletes, and more.

My mission is simple. Go! Make disciples…transform lives by pointing them to God and connecting them with others.

END NOTES

Note: The abbreviations below indicate the following publications:

NIV
Holy Bible, New International Version® (Grand Rapids, MI: Zondervan Publishing House, 1984).

NLT
Holy Bible, New Living Translation (Wheaton, IL: Tyndale House Publishers, Inc., 2004).

NASB
New American Standard Bible® (Anaheim, CA: Foundation Publications, 1995).

Message
The Message (Colorado Springs, CO: NavPress Publishing Group, 2002).

INTRODUCTION

[1] Galatians 5:1, *NIV*

[2] Galatians 5:1, *NIV*

[3] For more about my story, see my mini-bio at the back of the book.

[4] Luke 6:49, *Message*

[5] Romans 12:2, *NLT*

[6] Galatians 6:14-16, *Message*

[7] Galatians 2:19, *Message*

[8] Galatians 2:20, *Message*

[9] 1 Peter 4:1-2, *Message*

[10] James 4:13-15, *Message*

[11] Matthew 6:34, *Message*

[12] James 1:2-3, *Message*

[13] Romans 14:3-4, *Message*

[14] 1 Thessalonians 4:3, *NIV*

[15] *Holman's Bible Dictionary*, http://www.studylight.org/dic/hbd

[16] Romans 12:2, *NIV*

[17] 2 Corinthians 10:5, *NIV*

[18] 2 Corinthians 10:3, *The Message*

[19] Galatians 5:22, *NIV*

[20] The book *Minds On Fire* can be downloaded for free at LivesTransforming.com.

[21] 1 John 4:4, *NIV*

[22] John 8:44, *NIV*

[23] 1 John 5:6, *NIV*

[24] John 17:17, *NIV*

[25] *Holman's Bible Dictionary*, http://www.studylight.org/dic/hbd

[26] *Strong's Hebrew & Greek*, http://www.blueletterBible.org/lang/lexicon/lexicon.cfm?strongs=g3428t=kjv

CHAPTER 1

[27] John 8:36, *NIV*

[28] Mark 9:24, *NIV*

[29] Eph. 6:16, *NIV*

[30] Romans 8:1, *NASB*

[31] Acts 16:22, *NLT*

[32] Acts 16:25-31, *NLT*

[33] Romans 8:16, *Message*

[34] Galatians 6:14, *Message*

[35] Colossians 2:18-19, *Message*

[36] John 6:60, *NIV*

[37] Colossians 2:10, *NASB, emphasis mine*

[38] Romans 14:8-9, *Message, emphasis mine*

[39] Matthew 5:14, *Message, emphasis mine*

[40] 2 Corinthians 6:11, *Message, emphasis mine*

[41] Romans 7:20, *NAS, emphasis mine.*

[42] For a detailed discussion of this concept, especially in relation to the diagram, see Watchman Nee's *The Release of the Spirit* (New York: Christian Fellowship Publishers, Inc., 2000). "...for the purposes of this book, he has chosen to call man's spirit the *inner man*. He calls man's soul the *outer man*. And for the body he uses the term, the *outermost man*. In the diagram below we have pictured this.

It will also help us to realize that God, in designing man originally, intended for man's spirit to be His home or dwelling place. So the Holy Spirit, by making His union with the human spirit, was to govern the soul. Then further, the spirit through the soul would use the body as the means of expressing God's life and purpose" (p. 5).

[43] 2 Peter 1:13, *NIV*

[44] Romans 7:21-22, *NASB, emphasis mine*

[45] Romans 5:20-21, *Message*

[46] Romans 7:25, *NASB*

[47] 1 John 3:18-21, *Message, emphasis mine*

[48] Martin Luther, *The Freedom of a Christian* (Minneapolis, MN: Fortress, 2008), pp. 74-75.

[49] Romans 5:20-21, *Message*

CHAPTER 2

[50] Galatians 2:19, *Message*

[51] Galatians 2:19, *Message*

[52] Hebrews 7:11, *NIV*

[53] Galatians 3:21-22, *Message*

[54] Galatians 2:19-20, *Message*

[55] Romans 8:20, *NASB*

[56] Dave Burns, *Feeling Good: The New Mood Therapy* (New York: Avon Books, 1980), pp. 370-371.

[57] Galatians 2:19, *Message*

[58] Galatians 2:19-20, *Message*

[59] Galatians 3:11, *Message*

[60] Galatians 3:2-6, *Message*

[61] 1 John 4:17-18, *Message*

[62] Galatians 6:5, *Message*

CHAPTER 3

[63] Galatians 5:22-23, *NIV*

[64] Matthew 11:28-30, *Message*

[65] Psalm 139:13-14, *NIV*

[66] Luke 12:7, *NLT*

[67] Romans 2:23-24, *Message*

[68] Romans 5:1, *Message*

[69] Oswald Chambers, *The Complete Works of Oswald Chambers: If Thou Wilt Be Perfect: Talks on Spiritual Philosophy*, Ch. 4, "The Philosophy of Discernment" (Grand Rapids: Discovery House, 2000), p.p. 580-582.

[70] Ibid.

[71] Ibid.

[72] Ibid.

[73] Ibid.

[74] Ibid.

[75] Ibid.

[76] John 15:4-8, *Message, emphasis mine*

[77] Oswald Chambers, *My Utmost for His Highest* (Grand Rapids: Discovery House, 1992), August Ten.

CHAPTER 4

[78] Colossians 2:10, *NASB*

[79] Galatians 6:14-16, *Message*

[80] Romans 3:21-22; Romans 4:5, *NAS*

[81] Genesis 1:1, *NIV*

[82] 1 Peter 4:1-2, *Message, personalized*

[83] Genesis 3:4-6, *Message*

[84] Galatians 5:19, *NASB*

[85] Luke 4:5-8, *Message*

[86] Philippians 3:13, *NIV*

[87] Oswald Chambers, *The Complete Works of Oswald Chambers: Our Lord on How to Think* (Grand Rapids: Discovery House, 2000), p. 728.

[88] Colossians 2:10, *NASB*

[89] Luke 4:1-8, *NASB*

[90] 1 Peter 4:1-2, *Message*

[91] Research performed by Barna Group; published in multiple formats by Barna in 1999.

[92] http://atheism.about.com/od/atheistsfamiliesmarriage/a/athiestsdivorce.htm
also http://www.edivorcepapers.com/divorce-statistics/barna-divorce-statistics.html

[93] Mark 12:30, *NASB*

[94] Psalm 42:1, *NLT*

[95] Matthew 4: 1-11, *NASB*

[96] 1 Peter 4:1-2, *Message, personalized*

CHAPTER 5

[97] C. S. Lewis, *The Screwtape Letters* (San Francisco: Harper, 1996), p. 61.

[98] James 4, *Message*

[99] Matthew 6:34, *Message, emphasis mine*

[100] Matthew 6, *Message*

[101] Matthew 6, *Message*

[102] Romans 12:2, *NASB*

[103] 2 Corinthians 10:5, *NASB*

[104] Ephesians 6:16, *NASB*

[105] C.S. Lewis, *Screwtape Letters, pp. 61-62, emphasis mine*

[106] David Burns, *Feeling Good: The New Mood Therapy* (New York: Avon Books, 1980), p.p. 42-43.

[107] David Burns, *Feeling Good: The New Mood Therapy* (New York: Avon Books, 1980), p.p. 42-43.

[108] Matthew 6:34, *Message*

[109] Ibid.

[110] Matthew 6:30, *Message*

[111] Matthew 6:31-33, *Message*

[112] Romans 12:2, *NIV*

CHAPTER 6

[113] Ecclesiastes 8:14, *NLT*

[114] John 11:33-35, *NLT*

[115] Mark 11:15-16, *NIV*

[116] Mark 14:32-34, *NIV*

[117] 2 Corinthians 5:21, *NASB*

[118] John 16:33, *NIV*

[119] John 16:33, *NIV*

[120] Romans 5:3, *Message*

[121] Philippians 4:11-13, *NASB*

[122] James 1:2-4, *Message*

[123] Matthew 11:28-30, *Message*

[124] Romans 8:38-39, *NLT*

[125] James 1:2-4, *Message, emphasis mine*

[126] Romans 5:3-5, *Message, emphasis mine*

[127] Hebrews 12, *Message, emphasis mine*

[128] Romans 8:1, *NASB*

[129] John 16:33, *NIV*

[130] Hebrews 2:15, *Message, emphasis mine*

[131] Hebrews 2:15, *NASB*

CHAPTER 7

[132] John 8:4, 5, 7-11, *NLT*

[133] John 12:47, *NASB*

[134] 1 Peter 3:8-9, *Message*

[135] Colossians 4:5-6, *Message*

[136] Romans 14:4, *Message*

[137] Romans 14:13, *Message*

[138] Matthew 11:28, *NASB*

[139] Galatians 6:1-5, *Message*

[140] Romans 14:4, *Message*

[141] Matthew 7:1, *NASB* and Luke 6:37, *NASB*

[142] John 3:17, *NASB*

[143] John 12:47, *NASB*

[144] Romans 2:1, *NASB*

[145] James 4:12, *NASB*

[146] Romans 14:13, *NASB*

[147] 1 Corinthians 10:29, *NASB*

[148] Colossians 2:16, *NASB*

[149] James 2:4, *NASB*

[150] Luke 10:25-28, *Message*

[151] Galatians 2:20-21, *Message*

[152] Ephesians 5:1, *Message, emphasis mine*

[153] Romans 14:1, *NASB*

[154] Romans 14:13, *NASB*

[155] Mark 10:8-9, *NIV*

[156] Mark 10:11, *NIV*

[157] 1 Corinthians 9:20-22, *Message*